Why Is Jesus in the Microwave?

Funny Stories from Catholic Classrooms

Mary Kathleen Glavich, SND

Our Sunday Visitor Publishing Division
Our Sunday Visitor, Inc.
Huntington, Indiana 46750

Copyright © 2015 Sr. Mary Kathleen Glavich, SND. (Some of the text in this book appeared in *Catholic School Kids Say the Funniest Things*, by Mary Kathleen Glavich, SND [Paulist Press, 2002]). Cartoons copyright © 2015 Lucius Wisniewski. Published 2015.

20 19 18 17 16 15   1 2 3 4 5 6 7 8 9

ISBN: 978-1-61278-852-4 (Inventory No. T1656)
eISBN: 978-1-61278-857-9
LCCN: 2014958987

Cover design: Lindsey Riesen
Cover art: Shutterstock
Interior design: Sherri L. Hoffman
Interior art: Lucius Wisniewski

PRINTED IN THE UNITED STATES OF AMERICA

Dedicated to all those
Sisters of Notre Dame, who, proclaiming
God's goodness and provident care,
taught with passion, patience,
and a twinkle in their eyes.

Contents

Introduction

A cheerful heart is good medicine,
but a crushed spirit dries up the bones.
— Proverbs 17:22

Laughter, God's special gift to human beings, sets us apart from other creatures. Even laughing hyenas don't really laugh. Because we are made in God's image and likeness, it follows that God must have a sense of humor too! The fact that he created the platypus and two-year-olds proves it. In the Bible, God's lighter side is revealed early on by the joke he played on Sarah, Abraham's wife. When an angel foretold that this elderly couple would have a son, Sarah laughed at the news and became the unofficial patron saint of laughter. God had the last laugh, though, because Sarah did bear one-hundred-year-old Abraham a son (see Genesis 18:1-15; 21:1-7).

Jesus, the God-man, had a funny bone like the rest of us. Perhaps he was familiar with the Jewish proverb, "What soap is to the body, laughter is to the soul." Jesus conjures up ridiculous images: a camel trying to squeeze through the eye of a needle, a burning oil lamp placed under a bed, and a log in one's eye. No doubt Jesus chuckled when he sent the fisherman Peter to fetch tax money in a fish and when he told about the persistent woman who threatened to give a judge a black eye. Jesus even stooped to making a pun, which is lost in translation. He spoke of straining out a gnat (*galma*) and swallowing a camel (*gamla*).

Laughter has been called "the sound of the soul dancing" and "carbonated holiness." It expresses inner joy, one of the fruits of the Holy Spirit; and, according to the Jesuit Pierre Teilhard de Chardin, joy is the most infallible sign of the presence of God.

Laughter also has physical benefits. For good reasons it is known as the best (and cheapest) medicine. Laughing promotes health by massaging the inner organs, strengthening the immune system, improving blood flow, and relaxing muscles. It also releases endorphins, the feel-good hormones that reduce stress and pain. Ironically, like a disease, laughter is contagious.

The Origin of This Book

This small book is a collection of humorous anecdotes gleaned from the classrooms of the Sisters of Notre Dame. For more than 140 years, we have been in the United States, carrying out the spiritual work of mercy "teaching the ignorant." This challenging work has been brightened by the amusing things that students, parents, and we ourselves have done.

Children are a constant source of laughter, as any parent knows. The surprising things they say and do keep the show *America's Funniest Home Videos* in business. Many times during a school day, we teachers struggle to keep a straight face, and failing that, burst out in laughter, what comedian Milton Berle called "an instant vacation."

The anecdotes in this book cover misunderstandings, mispronunciations, and mistakes in various subject areas. The students range from preschool to high school age. Some humble sisters tell on themselves, recounting blunders they made. The merry tales found on these pages prove that truth is funnier than fiction.

I guarantee that as you read them, you will smile, if not laugh out loud.

Why Is Jesus in the Microwave? is a warm, enjoyable treat that makes the perfect gift for anyone associated with Catholic schools or looking for funny stories to add spice to a homily or talk. We must teach laughter to a world that has many reasons not to laugh. Isn't this the point of Pope Francis' apostolic exhortation *The Joy of the Gospel?*

The little prince in Antoine de Saint-Exupéry's *The Little Prince* leaves his friend the gift of his laughter. To whom can you give that gift today?

Working with children, young and old, we sisters are laughing all the way to heaven! I invite you to join us. Go ahead. Indulge in a little laughter.

Mary Kathleen Glavich, SND
September 18, 2014
Feast of St. Joseph of Cupertino
(known for physical levity)

1. Religion

"Why does Father put Jesus into the microwave?"

The Microwave?

At a certain parish, the tabernacle was a wide rectangular box set into the wall. One day the primary children were learning about the Mass. At the end of the lesson, Sister asked, "Does anyone have any questions?"

With furrowed brow, a child inquired, "Why does Father put Jesus into the microwave?"

The Fourth Person

The pastor posed a trick question to the students he was visiting. God is eternal and had no beginning, but Father asked, "Who is the oldest — God the Father, God the Son, or God the Holy Spirit?"

The first child to answer said, "God the Father."

A second child asked, "God the Son?"

A third child guessed, "The Holy Spirit."

After replying no to all three answers, feigning exasperation, Father asked, "Doesn't anybody know who the oldest is?"

Then a timid voice queried, "Is Amen the oldest?"

A Papal Error

Sister Sharon proved that teachers are not infallible. When she informed her second-graders that Pope Benedict XV had resigned, immediately one boy's hand shot up. He commented, "Last year when I was in the first grade, he was Pope Benedict XVI."

A Handy Shopping List

During a religion lesson, Sister Barbara presented her eighth-graders with a unique question. She said, "You are always writing reminders to yourselves on your hands. Suppose Jesus did this. What might he write on his hand?"

One student in all seriousness proposed, "Buy soap for the washing of the feet."

Who's Confused?

The third-graders were reviewing the gifts God gave our first parents. There was one more gift to mention — namely, infused knowledge. "What gift is missing?" Sister asked.

Martin's face lit up, and he waved his hand excitedly. "Martin?"

The boy stood and proudly stated, "God gave Adam and Eve confused knowledge."

A Good Guess

Sister Elizabeth gave her class a quiz on the coming of Jesus to earth as a man. One child was weak in theology but strong in logic. In answer to the question "When the angel asked Mary to be the Mother of God, what did she say?" he had written, "Why me?"

Forbidden Dentures

The pastor was checking to see whether the first-graders remembered the previous lesson he had taught. Unfortunately, he called on Christina, who had been absent for that lesson. He asked her to recite the First Commandment. In response to her blank look, Father gave the child a helpful start. He prompted, "I am the Lord your God."

No response.

Again he tried, "I am the Lord your God. You shall not …"

Still no response.

Yet again, "I am the Lord your God. You shall not have false …"

This time Christina's face lit up. "Teeth?" she asked hopefully.

P for Perplexing

Sister Barbara was discussing the last days of Jesus with the first-graders. "Jesus went to Jerusalem for a special feast day. What was it? It begins with *p*."

"St. Patrick's Day!" one youngster volunteered.

"No," replied Sister.

Another child raised his hand. "Thanksgiving," he said.

In a scornful voice, a classmate commented, "What a dumb answer. The pilgrims never went to Jerusalem."

Guest Appearance

As a family with a small boy was walking by the school chapel, the mother said, "Let's make a visit to Jesus." Inside the chapel, the mother pointed to the tabernacle and whispered to her son, "Jesus is in there."

Curious, the boy whispered back, "When's he coming out?"

Mixed Vegetables

Father was reviewing the story of Our Lord's passion with the children. He asked, "What was the name of the garden Jesus and his apostles went to after the Last Supper?"

A boy raised his hand and waved it wildly. He was not one who usually knew the answers.

"Do you really know?" asked a surprised Father.

"Yes," said the boy confidently. "The Garden of Pickles."

"Close," granted the priest.

A God Like Jonah

Melinda was quite impressed with her teacher's revelation that God dwelt within her. That evening at dinner she shared this information with her parents. Then she swallowed a spoonful of peas and commented, "When those peas get down to my stomach and God tastes them, he'll say, 'Oh, Melinda. I just love peas.'"

The Ultimate Evil

Father presumed that the first-graders knew a lot of theology. "Does anyone know who the leader of the bad angels was?" he asked. Sister was surprised to see one little boy's hand shoot up.

"Yes?" Father asked.

"The boogeyman," the boy declared emphatically.

Ending with a Bang

While visiting the second-grade class, Father invited the children to ask him questions. One lad raised his hand and asked, "Father, do you really believe that Jesus is in the tabernacle?"

"Why, yes," Father replied.

"Do you *really* believe that Jesus is in the tabernacle?" the youngster persisted.

"Yes," Father repeated.

"Then why do you slam the door of the tabernacle?" the boy asked innocently.

From that day on, Father always closed the tabernacle door gently.

Morale Support for a Bishop

To welcome the new bishop, Sister Josephmarie invited the students in her school to write him letters. At the end of the day, among the letters piled on her desk she found an intimate one from a fourth-grader. It read, "Now I know you are a new bishop and so you are probably very nervous. But don't be. I'll tell you a secret. I'm praying for you."

Omnipresence

"Do you know where God is?" Sister asked her first-graders.

One boy confidently answered, "In our bathroom."

Curious, Sister inquired, "How do you know?"

"Because every morning my dad pounds on the door and asks, 'My God, are you still in there?'"

Experiential Lesson

Carrying out the God Lab lesson with her new, challenging high school class, Sister Dion found out just how different the students were from others she had taught. For the first project, the students were to create something out of play dough. As one boy worked, he commented, "I'm making a devil, and I'm naming it Dion."

The students set their creations on the teacher's desk. Next the lesson plan called for the teacher to smash the work to illustrate how sin destroys creation. Previous students had always calmly absorbed the lesson. However, this time, as Sister began crushing their masterpieces, the students rebelled. The room was in an uproar. One boy called out, "You murderess."

Sister never forgot, or repeated, the lesson.

The Living Dead

Assuming her students learned about vocations in previous years, Sister Bernadel asked them to name the states in life. One seventh-grader supplied the answer, "There are three states in life: religious, married, and dead."

Trapped

While studying about religious life, the eighth-graders encountered the word *cloister*. Sister explained, "A cloister is a monastery where outsiders do not enter and the religious usually do not leave."

On hearing this, Dan, the class clown, quipped, "Gee, Sister, don't they get cloisterphobia?"

A Promotion

Father Paul visited the kindergarten class for the first time. He asked, "Does anyone know my name?"

"I know. I know," one child replied with exuberance. "It's John Paul II."

Mary, a U.S. Citizen!

The sixth-graders were practicing for a May crowning. Luckily, the lad reading the Gospel passage about the Annunciation had the chance to be corrected. He proclaimed that the angel Gabriel was sent to a Virginian betrothed to a man named Joseph.

2. The Bible

"Jesus was walking along. He saw ten men who were very sick. Umm ... they had a bad disease.... They were all leprechauns!"

Divine Tricks

Sister finished telling her first-graders the marvelous story of creation according to Genesis. Awed by the account, a little fellow concluded, "Gee, God must be a magician!"

The First Stork Story

The fourth-graders were studying the story of Adam and Eve. One thoughtful boy asked Sister Helen Louise, "Were Adam and Eve the only two people around?"

"Yes," Sister replied.

"And did Eve have a baby?" the boy continued.

"Yes."

Perplexed, the boy asked, "Then who cut the vocal cord?"

Bible Bungle

While correcting her third-graders' tests, Sister Mary came upon this unique description of Moses: a man who took a man and woman of every kind on a boat.

A Major Mistake

In religion class, Sister Margaret asked her high school students, "What is the difference between the Major and Minor Prophets?"

There was a long silence. No one seemed to remember that the four Major Prophets were the ones who wrote the longest prophetic books in the Bible.

Finally, one student who knew something of Scripture guessed, "The major ones were there at the Resurrection, and the minor ones were hiding in the Upper Room."

Accurate Records

Mike, a sixth-grader, was enlightened one day when Sister Bernadel explained that the Scripture reference Isaiah 7:14 stood for the book of Isaiah, chapter 7, verse 14. He confessed, "I thought that 7:14 meant the time Isaiah made the prophecy."

Catholics in the Temple

One of Sister Anelle's students read the Bible with a modern mind. He wondered why Jesus chased people out of the Temple for playing Bingo.

Irish Expats in Israel

Charlie, a fourth-grader, was retelling his favorite Bible story to his classmates. He began, "Jesus was walking along. He saw ten men who were very sick."

He paused, trying to recall what was wrong with the men. "Umm, umm … they had a bad disease."

Suddenly his face brightened. "They were all leprechauns!" he declared triumphantly.

Like the Cheshire Cat

One child knew the comic strips better than he knew the Bible. When Sister asked, "What was the name of the angel who appeared to Mary at the time of the Annunciation?" this student answered, "Garfield."

Old Testament Fairy Tales

Sister Barbara's sixth-grade CCD class was reviewing some Old Testament stories. In recounting the story of Joshua's victory at the battle of Jericho, one lad got his tales mixed up. He said, "The Israelites surrounded the town of Jericho. Then they huffed and they puffed, and they blew the walls down."

Then There's the Pumpkin Eater

Sister Colette was about to tell her first-graders a Gospel story about Jesus and the apostle Peter. To introduce the story, she asked, "Does anyone know who Peter was?"

One boy timidly raised his hand and answered with a lisp, "I think he wath a wabbit."

St. Paul's Tenth Missionary Journey?

Sister Barbara was telling the kindergarteners stories about St. Paul. She explained how he traveled a lot, visiting Christian churches. "Did he come to Newbury?" asked one little boy, whose church was St. Helen's in Newbury, Ohio.

3. The Mass

"Jesus on a stick?"

An Altered View

A little boy asked his teacher, "Before Mass starts, why does Father smell the altar?"

Holy Smokes!

During a school Mass, incense was used. On the way back to the classroom, a student unfamiliar with Catholic rites remarked to Sister Domicele, "Father Paul is a good cook."

Terminology

Sister Brian was introducing the first-graders to some of the items used during Mass. She held up the processional cross, a pole topped by a crucifix that is carried at the head of the entrance procession.

"Does anyone know what this is?" Sister asked.

A youngster's hand flew up, and she ventured a guess. "Jesus on a stick?"

A Logical Answer

A visiting priest from Uganda was presiding at a school Mass. During the homily he asked, "Does anyone know where I come from?"

One child raised his hand and answered, "China."

The priest's eyebrows shot up. "China? Why do you say that?"

"Well, everything comes from China," the boy explained matter-of-factly.

An Early Responsorial Verse

At Mass, the first reading was the passage from Corinthians where St. Paul enumerates his sufferings as an apostle. Father read how Paul was imprisoned, whipped, beaten, stoned, shipwrecked, in danger from eight things, sleepless, hungry, cold, and naked. Suddenly a boy in the front row loudly blurted out, "Wow! What a guy!"

The priest dryly replied, "Well, at least one person is listening to the reading."

Good Discipline

Sister Mary Adelle was perturbed. During Father's homily at the school Mass, one of her second-graders in the front row was talking and fooling around. Not wanting to cause a disturbance by walking to the front, Sister just leaned forward and in a loud whisper said, "Neil!"

Immediately her whole class knelt. One by one the other classes followed suit until the whole student body was kneeling.

Intercession for Life

The second-graders were gathered for a school Mass. A child who was new to the school walked in late and sat at the end of the first pew. He had been to the practice for the liturgy, so he had some idea of the ritual. When it came time for the prayer of the faithful, he marched up to the lectern and prayed a spontaneous intercession: "For the birds and the bees, let us pray to the Lord."

Fidelity

One day dignitaries from the Notre Dame community joined the school for its weekly Mass. The second-grade teacher was concerned because the student who was to read the responsorial psalm had not arrived. To remedy the situation, Sister asked her best reader to substitute.

At the appointed time, the substitute walked up to the lectern and proclaimed the responsorial verse: "The fiddle-dee-dee of the Lord remains forever."

The whole school, including the eighth-graders, calmly repeated this refrain … and continued to repeat it to the end of the psalm.

Making Peace

The first-graders were at the school Mass for the first time. After the sign of peace, Sister noticed that five-year-old Michael was rubbing his eyes. She thought he might be crying. She walked up to his pew, and, sure enough, tears were running down the little boy's face.

"What's wrong, Michael?" she asked.

"Nobody shook my hand," he said with a sniff. Sister shook his hand.

Words from on High

The junior-high students were in their classroom practicing a song for Mass. They sang, "Is there any word from the Lord?" A second later the principal's voice sounded over the PA system: "Good morning, teachers, girls, and boys. Today I would like to say a few words to you about snow."

The Mute Button

During a rather long homily at a school Mass, a boy in the front row of Sister's class was talking. To avoid a commotion, Sister whispered to the child sitting beside her, "Go up there and tell him to stop talking."

The child dutifully walked down the aisle and stopped in front of the lectern. Looking up at the priest, he declared: "Sister said you should stop talking."

Liturgy Pageant

A deacon was giving the homily at a school Mass. He pointed to the stole crossed over his left shoulder and questioned, "Does anyone know what this means?" Immediately a first-grade girl raised her hand. Sister whispered to her, "Put your hand down. You don't know."

"Yes, I do," the girl declared.

"No, you don't," Sister argued.

"Yes, I do," the girl insisted.

The deacon said, "Little girl who's making such a fuss, what does this stole mean?"

Loud and clear the girl proclaimed, "Miss America!"

Hearing Things

The school was gathered in church waiting for Mass to begin. One of the fourth-graders walked back to her teacher and held out a ring. She said, "Sister, someone left this in the first 'pewk.'"

Father's Little Confessor

Before an early morning Mass, the priest — a friend of Sister Kathleen — was waiting for the missing altar server. Just as Father was about to walk into the sanctuary, the tardy lad appeared.

"Well, you can just join the congregation now," the priest said to the server.

"But, Father," the boy remonstrated, "who will wash you of your iniquity and cleanse you of your sin?"

4. Sacraments and Sacramentals

"Sister, is my medal blessed, or must I take it home and soak it in holy water?"

Education Gap

In preparing her second-graders for the Sacrament of Reconciliation, Sister Karlene taught them about penance. She explained, "Father might say to you, 'For your penance, say five Our Fathers.'"

After the students filed out of the room, one little boy remained at his desk crying. When Sister asked the reason for his tears, he sobbed, "I only know one Our Father, not the other four."

Saturated with Grace

At a religious-goods sale, a second-grader bought a medal on a chain. Concerned that it be a real sacramental, he asked, "Sister, is my medal blessed, or must I take it home and soak it in holy water?"

Branded

A new fourth-grade student, who had never experienced Ash Wednesday before, nervously asked his teacher, "Are the ashes hot?"

Future Priest

Father was having Benediction for the school. When it was time for the blessing, the inexperienced altar boy did not move to get the cope.

"The cope," Father prompted.

The boy walked over to the cope, picked it up, and wrapped it around his own shoulders.

A Lesson That Got Home

Mr. and Mrs. Brown took turns driving the sisters to teach CCD on Saturdays. One morning Mrs. Brown told this story:

She and Mr. Brown were having a discussion. At one point, the conversation was becoming a little heated. Suddenly, little Suzie, who had recently made her First Confession, interrupted.

"Daddy," she said, "now you apologize to Mommy!"

Quite taken aback, Mr. Brown asked, "Why?"

Suzie explained, "Because you started an argument with Mommy."

Mr. Brown then apologized. But little Suzie was not going to let her father off so easily. In a serious tone she continued, "Daddy, you know it's not enough to just say you're sorry. You have to try really hard never to do it again."

"That does it," said Mr. Brown. "Next week the sisters walk to school!"

According to Hoyle

The confirmandi had been told that during the ceremony they were to hand their name cards to the priest next to the bishop and he would return them. The first child stood before the bishop and was solemnly confirmed, but the assisting priest failed to return his card. Determined to follow the rubrics, the lad informed the priest and everyone within hearing, "But Sister said you should give it back to me."

Smart Girl

Sister Marthe overheard some children acting out a wedding. The priest asked the bride, "Do you take him for better or worse?"

"For better," the little girl said quickly.

The priest continued, "For richer or poorer?"

"For richer," stated the miniature bride.

Giving Credit Where Credit's Due

Three-year-old Jonathan came in to talk to Sister Joann, while his father, another teacher, was working in his classroom. Jonathan confessed to Sister that right before they came, he had not obeyed his parents. They were very angry and were going to spank him, but they didn't.

"My, you were lucky!" Sister commented.

"Lucky! Not lucky! I was blessed!" Jonathan imme-diately corrected.

A Mystery

The fourth-graders were reviewing the mysteries of the Rosary. When they got to the sorrowful mysteries, Sister called on a child to name the fourth mystery. He responded, "The scorching at the pillar."

5. Prayer

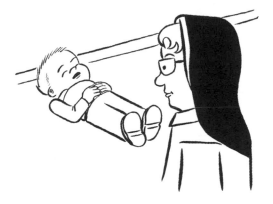

"OK, Sister, I'm ready to say my night prayers for you."

Sneaking Up on Jesus

A teacher en route to church with her small students reminded them to walk quietly so that they wouldn't disturb other classes. She urged, "Try to be so quiet that even Jesus won't know we're coming."

The children obeyed conscientiously. They tiptoed to the church, and one child quietly opened the door. As the first little ones entered the church, suddenly a little girl gleefully shouted, "Surprise!"

First-Century Planes

The school was assembled in the gym for the Stations of the Cross. A special microphone system had been set up. Everyone was finally in place and hushed, waiting for the Lenten devotion to begin. A first-grader was the first one to the microphone. In a strong voice he announced, "The First Station, the pilot said Jesus must die!"

Heaven's Housing Policy

Sister Laurann was proud that she had taught her young students to begin the day with petitions for the world's needs. She doubted her success, however, when one morning a lad earnestly prayed, "That God will change his mind about letting dogs go to heaven, let us pray to the Lord."

Divine Affirmation

During the first-graders' religion class, Sister Ann invited, "Now let's close our eyes and listen to what God is saying to us."

It was very quiet as the children prayed silently. After a short time, Sister asked, "Can anyone tell us what God said to them?"

One hand went up, and a small boy reported, "Kevin, you're my best invention."

Semi-Contrition

A second-grader preparing for First Reconciliation was practicing the Act of Contrition. He began, "O my God, I am partly sorry...."

A Mystified Pray-er

The senior class was on retreat at the sisters' provincial center. The retreat director encouraged them to spend as much time as possible in the chapel.

Later, one girl reported to the principal that she had a hard time praying. She said, "After a while I ran out of things to say. But every time I went back to the chapel, the same little old sisters were there. What could they find to say after praying for so many years?"

A Happy Ending

When November 2 came along, the second-graders learned about the poor souls in purgatory. At least one child remembered the lesson — at least partially. A few days later during the morning prayers of petition, Andrea prayed, "For the repose of the soul of my uncle. He was killed in a car accident but is doing much better now."

Rote Prayers

Despite the school rule that no children may enter the building during recess, one day two young girls appeared at the principal's office very excited. They announced, "Sister Regina, we saw the Blessed Virgin above the garages."

"Is that so? Did you tell the teacher out there?" Sister asked.

"Yes," the girls shook their heads. "She saw Mary too."

Deciding that this needed to be investigated, Sister Regina went outside and walked over to the teacher.

"Yes," the teacher confirmed, "some clouds were in the shape of the Blessed Virgin."

Turning to the two girls, Sister Regina asked, "What did you do when you saw Mary?"

"Well," one girl replied, "we said our First Communion prayers, then we prayed a Hail Mary, and then we said the Pledge of Allegiance to the Flag."

A Fan

In the school chapel there was a book in which the students recorded petitions. To the amusement of the faculty, one petition read, "That Sister Mary Judith Ann may continue to teach."

The Lord's Sabbath

The students were writing acrostic prayers to God based on their names. Each letter in their name began a phrase of their prayer. Maurene's prayer was quite unusual. For one E in her name she had written, "Eternal rest grant unto you, O Lord."

A Parent's Prank?

Sister Thomasin told her third-graders that for homework they were to bring to school pictures of people they should pray for. To her surprise, one student came with a picture of Lady Godiva.

Greeting Gabriel

Sister asked her first-graders what Mary said when the angel appeared to her. A quick-thinking lad answered, "She probably said, 'Angel of God, my guardian dear.'"

It's All Relative

When praying intercessory prayers, Sister Regina's fourth-graders prayed only for family members and pets. To teach the children to make their intentions more inclusive, Sister decided to act as a model. She began to offer prayers such as "For all police officers and firefighters who work to keep us safe" and "For people in hospitals and those who try to bring them back to good health."

One day Sister asked, "Does anyone notice that my prayers are different from everyone else's?" Heads nodded vigorously.

"How are they different?" Sister asked.

Mark responded, "Well, we all pray for our relatives. But you don't seem to have any."

Eager Beaver

On the first day of school, Sister Harold explained the daily routine. She said, "When I tap the bell, we'll all stand and say a little prayer."

A voice rang out, "Sister, don't make it two decades, just one. I want to get going."

Prayer Posture

The first-graders were talking about prayer. Johnny informed everyone that he prayed every night. "Can you say your night prayers for me?" Sister Mary de Xavier asked.

The boy thought for a while and then asked, "Can I get on the floor?"

"Sure," Sister replied.

Johnny got down on the floor, lay on his back, and folded his hands on his chest. Then he recited his night prayers.

False Alarm

Whenever fire engine sirens were heard during a lesson, Sister Ricarda and her students prayed for the firefighters and the people in danger. Sister discovered that this practice had made quite an impression on the children after she taught them the prayer for the faithful departed, who may be enduring the fires of purgatory.

One day she was surprised to hear some children praying, "Eternal rest grant unto them, O Lord, and let perpetual light shine upon them. May their souls and the souls of all the fire department, through the mercy of God, rest in peace. Amen."

Messages from Heaven

After a time of quiet prayer, Sister Marie asked her first-graders what God had said to them.

A child answered, "God told me he loves me."

Another said, "God said, 'Thank you for coming to Sunday school.'"

To one child, God sounded just like her parents. She said, "God told me to turn down the TV."

6. Saints

"Sister, where are you in the picture?"

St. Charade

One eighth-grader refused to take notes as his class viewed filmstrips on the lives of the saints. He insisted to Sister Andrew that he could remember the material. Later a quiz proved him wrong when he made these identifications: St. Martian Despress (for Martin de Porres) — He cured people and then they died;

St. Catherine of Siena — She cut off her hair, and then she became a noun.

Living Saint

Sister Mary Beth took her first-graders to the church for a tour. The children stood in awe before the large, colorful stained-glass window that depicted Pentecost. It showed the Holy Spirit coming down upon Mary and the apostles. One child whispered seriously, "Sister, where are you in the picture?"

Modern Translation

The seventh grade was telling the story of John the Baptist's life. When it came to the part where John declared that he was not worthy to unloose the Savior's sandals, one student gave an original version. He stated, "John said he wasn't worthy to untie Christ's saddle shoes."

Mary's New Vocation

Two kindergarten students were discussing whether or not the Blessed Virgin Mary was a sister.

"She had to be a sister. She wore a veil," said one.

"No, she was St. Joseph's wife and had a baby, Jesus," retorted the other.

"Well, after Jesus and St. Joseph died, then she became a sister," explained the first.

"Yeah, that's probably true," conceded the second.

A Tableau

In the front yard of St. Joan of Arc Church stands a large, white marble statue of St. Joan astride a horse. One fall day when Sister looked out the window, she saw that figures had been added to the scene. Two third-grade boys stood, one on either side of St. Joan, sticks drawn as swords, pledging their loyalty to the warrior-saint.

Saint Defaming

As homework to prepare for the Solemnity of All Saints, Sister Jude Andrew told her children to learn something about their patron saints. On the feast day itself, the parish priest paid a visit. Father asked little Frank, "Who is your patron?"

"St. Francis," came the quick reply, to Sister's relief.

"Good," said Father. "Do you know anything about your patron saint?"

"Oh, yes, Father," Frank said. "He was a sissy."

Food for Thought

Before the Solemnity of All Saints, the first- and second-graders were discussing heaven. Lacey said, "There must be an awfully long table in heaven for all those people. And it's going to take forever to pass the mashed potatoes."

Alex tried to dispel her concerns. He said, "I heard that our plates will be full when they are put in front of us."

Not one to stop worrying, Lacey replied, "But what will we do for seconds?"

Clean Spirits

One little girl was spending a very long time in the bathtub. Puzzled, her mother questioned, "Why are you in there for so long, honey?"

"I'm washing my guardian angel" was the surprising reply.

The next day the girl came home from school and

announced to her mother's relief, "Mom, I don't have to worry about my guardian angel anymore. I found out that he doesn't have a body."

Jumping to Conclusions

After showing the third-graders a video about St. Joseph, Sister Judy asked them to write what they learned about this great saint. To her surprise, one child wrote, "St. Joseph decided to divorce Mary because he thought she was having an affair."

7. Morality

"I'd never do that!"

The Last Word

After a heavy snowfall, two little boys built a snow fort during recess. Later, while they were at lunch, one boy announced, "I'm going to eat fast so I can play in my fort."

The other boy countered, "That's my fort. I thought of it."

Quite a little argument followed until one boy concluded, "Well, it's really God's snow."

The Truthful Liar

The seventh-graders were discussing honesty. One boy frankly explained, "I don't believe in stealing or lying because you break the commandments. I wouldn't steal anything because I would offend God and Mary. I don't steal. Maybe I lie a little bit, but nobody's perfect."

A Fifty-Fifty Chance?

Sister encouraged her children to prepare their hearts for Christ's coming at Christmas by being good. She also explained the need for being ready for his coming on the last day. Christ will judge people, and those who were good will go to live with him in heaven.

Little Chris became thoughtful. Finally he raised his hand and asked, "What if you are half good and half bad? What happens then?"

A Dirty Word

Sister Julie, the school secretary, was interrupted one day by a little boy. "Sister, Jimmy said a bad word," he reported.

"He did? What did Jimmy say?"

"I can't tell you. It's a bad word, and I'm not supposed to say it."

"But if you don't tell me what it was, I can't teach Jimmy."

"OK. I'll whisper it to you."

With that, the tattletale leaned toward Sister's ear and whispered, "Asphalt."

Pleading Innocent

The preschool children were playing "Who Stole the Cookies from the Cookie Jar?" in order to learn one another's names. One by one, children were named and accused in the game. At one point, someone chose Brian for a turn by chanting, "Brian stole the cookies from the cookie jar."

Brian began to cry and said, "I'd never do that." It took a while to convince him that it was only a game.

Revenge

The second-graders were talking about the virtues of Jesus and how we could imitate him.

Sister said, "When people hurt you, act like Jesus. Give them another chance. Forgive them." Then she asked, "But what if the person who hurts you is really mean and doesn't like you at all? Think: What would Jesus do then?"

The answer came quickly: "He'd send them straight to hell."

Turning Up the Heat

During the severe winter months of 1977, a gas shortage made it difficult to heat the schools. The children of St. Mary's had to share a building with the neighboring public school, Avon East. One public school teacher prepared her students to welcome the children from St. Mary's. After she finished, one boy raised his hand. He wanted to inform his classmates about what to expect.

"You know what?" he said seriously. "The children from the Catholic school are really different from us. If I would hit one of them on the cheek, he would turn the other cheek."

Hearing about this description, the sisters at St. Mary's prayed, "Dear God, please don't let any of our children be put to the test."

8. Reading

A Good Try

During a phonics game, Mary said, "I'm thinking of a word that begins with the letter *G*."

"Are you thinking of the word *Jesus*?" asked Frank.

"Jesus begins with *J*," Mary replied.

Then Bette guessed, "Are you thinking of the word *God*?"

Frank immediately challenged, "But isn't Jesus God?"

"Yes," answered Mary, "but God spells his name with a *G*."

A Rose by Any Other Name

One lad who attended a small rural school must not have been helping Dad with the farm work. When it was his turn to read from the textbook, he evoked gales of laughter from the class by saying "MAN your ray," for the substance used as fertilizer.

All-Purpose Room

Sister Barbara was preparing her fourth-graders to read a story in which the parlor of a house was mentioned. Realizing that many of the children would be unfamiliar with the word *parlor*, Sister Barbara asked, "What is a parlor?"

Vince replied, "Where you're either laid out or get your hair cut."

A Multiplication of Tables

The second-graders had just received new textbooks. Intending to give the class an overview of what was in their books, Sister Mary announced, "Boys and girls, I'd like you to turn to the table of contents." To her surprise, the children turned around in their desks and looked at the table in the back of the room.

A Close Call

First-year teacher Sister Mary Bruce was concerned about a story in her reader. One of the characters was a dog named Wee Brucie. Not looking forward to being called Wee Brucie by her children for the rest of the year, Sister asked the principal for a different set of readers. No, the school couldn't afford another set.

The day finally arrived when the dreaded story was

to be read. The boy who was reading aloud came to the sentence that introduced Wee Brucie. He pronounced the name "Wee Brucky." No one batted an eye or corrected him — including Sister. Throughout the story, the children called the dog "Brucky."

A Haven in Distress

Sister Pamela, a principal, received a note from a teacher that read, "Nathan left for the washroom and has not come back." Upon arriving at the boys' washroom, Sister found that the outside doors, which were usually open, were closed and the lights were off. She called, "Nathan are you here?"

"Yes, Sister," came the answer.

"Do you feel all right?"

"Yes, Sister."

"Your teacher is worried about you," Sister said. "When are you going back to the classroom?"

"Is phonics almost over?"

A Secret Romance

In reading class, the first-graders were reviewing words on flashcards. Victor got the word *kiss*. He read it and commented, "That's a nice word."

Another boy announced, "I know why. It's because he loves Terrie."

Victor blushed and looked embarrassed. Then he said, "Aw, and I was keeping it a secret for so many days."

Grave Labels

The parish elementary school in the countryside was near a cemetery. One day a young student commented to his teacher, "A lot of those tombstones have really strange words on them. They say, 'Died rich.'"

After school, Sister walked over to the cemetery to see what the child was talking about. She discovered that buried in the graveyard were many members of the Diederich family.

A Couple of Meanings

The primary-grade children were reading a story about hats. When Sister came to the line that referred to hats for brides and hats for grooms, she asked, "What's a groom?"

One child answered brightly, "That's when your dog gets a haircut."

Just Following Directions

At the beginning of the school year, Sister Sharon noticed that Jeremy, one of her second-graders, was in the hall. Suddenly, the fire alarm sounded. "This is a strange time to have a fire drill," Sister thought.

Then she realized that the fire alarm was in the hall. She looked out the door. No Jeremy. Quickly, Sister called the office to report that it was a false alarm. She asked the secretary to make a PA announcement telling Jeremy to go to his classroom.

A few minutes later, Jeremy emerged from the chapel. Why had he set off the fire alarm? Well, he read the words on the bar, "Pull down."

9. English

"Sister, what was that ZIP code again?"

Multilingual?

"Sister, my baby brother knows three languages," a first-grade girl declared.

Curious, Sister Ann asked, "Oh, really? What are they?"

"Mother," "Father," and "good-bye," the girl proudly stated.

A Fun House

Patty, a fifth-grader, was eager to learn what to expect in her new school.

"Will we go on any field trips?" she asked Sister Mary.

"Oh, yes," her teacher replied.

Then Patty proudly informed her, "In my other school, our teacher took our whole class to the hysterical museum."

Pronounced Mispronunciations

The English class was studying the play *A Long Day's Journey into Night*. In reading a section aloud, one innocent girl kept repeating that the characters were going to the "ba-ROOM," instead of the barroom. Later, as the class discussed the play, another student mentioned how afraid Ben was, fearing that he was going to be sent to the "ASS-lum."

For the rest of the year, the class enjoyed saying, "If you don't behave, you will be sent to the ba-ROOM or the ASS-lum."

A Sketchy Understanding

All week Sister Dismas had taught development lessons on character study. On Friday, for a culminating activity, she asked the students to do a character sketch. Later, as she was grading the compositions, Sister found that one student had neatly drawn a character on his notebook paper.

A Neat Blend Word

Sister always insisted that the classroom had to be kept clean. Unused to such tidiness, one student commented, "Gee, Sister, you sure are persnicular."

A Mistake

The children were playing on the playground during recess. All at once little Johnny came crying to Sister. He sobbed, "Bobby hit me under the fire mistake."

A Good Try

A six-year-old began, "Sister, this summer me and Sabrina …"

Sister interrupted, "No, honey, it's Sabrina and I."

The girl's mouth fell open. Excitedly she asked, "Oh, were you there too?"

Improving English

Reviewing figures of speech with her eighth-graders, Sister Andrew asked, "What is an exaggeration called?" Hoping to hear the answer "hyperbole," Sister was surprised but tickled when a student responded, "Hyperbomb."

The Babbling Student

As a biology project, one tenth-grade girl taped nature sounds. Her finished product was quite good — except for the part that played gurgling water. The girl had labeled it "A Babbling Crook."

Girded for War

Sister Luke explained to her college English students that the knights of yore were dedicated to a lady. They wore an item of their lady, such as a handkerchief or a sash, tied on to their arm or helmet. This token, called a favor, reminded them that they fought in her honor.

In the story "Sir Gawain and the Green Knight," Gawain receives a red waistband, or girdle, from a lady. That day Sister confused this story with *Idylls of the*

King, in which Lancelot receives a sleeve from Elaine. To her class's delight, she concluded, "And that is why Sir Lancelot went into battle with Elaine's girdle on."

Living in a Glass House

Kevin and Peter lined up at Sister Cupertino's desk to ask questions. "Sister, should we do our paper in cursing?" Kevin asked.

Startled, Sister asked, "What, Kevin?"

"Should we do our paper in cursing writing?" the boy clarified.

"Oh, you mean cursive writing," Sister corrected. "Yes. Do it in cursive."

As Kevin walked away, Peter stepped up and leaned confidentially on the desk. Casting a look of pity at Kevin, he said, "Boy, Sister, he can't repounce anything!"

Misnomer

As the first-graders were walking through the junior-high hall, one young fellow remarked, "I don't know why they call this a high hall. It's no higher than our hall."

Daffynition

Sister Barbara gives Mike credit for creative thinking. When she asked, "What is an aqueduct?" he answered, "It's something like a seal but has webbed feet."

Casting Your Bread

The fourth-graders were talking about the Olympics. One child happily contributed to the discussion by telling about the "biscuit thrower" event.

A *Unique* Pronunciation

Sister Francetta's Latin students took a test on English words derived from Latin. Afterwards, as the class was filing out of the room, one girl asked a friend, "Hey, Di, what did you put for 'OO knee kway'?"

With Mom's Approval

The students turned in essays on *Catcher in the Rye*. One essay was suspicious. It was not written in the style of the student and was curiously free of spelling errors. Did the girl use Cliff Notes? No. She used Monarch Notes, copying the opening paragraphs verbatim. When Sister Mary Kathleen met with the plagiarizer after school, she began, "About your essay …"

"My mom thought it was really good," the girl broke in.

"Did she know you copied it?" Sister asked.

"My mom liked it," the girl insisted. Then she said in defense, "I changed three words."

"Yes, and you added a period that created an incomplete sentence!"

Com-moo-nicating

Sister Mary Leola taught English in a rural high school. On the first day of school, she explained to the juniors that they could expect to write a great deal during the year. She encouraged them to have a positive attitude, commenting, "Everyone has a lot to say."

With that, as if on cue, the Black Angus cows across the road began to moo.

A Huge Problem

One day Sister Mary Claire directed her first- and second-graders to write about any story they wished and draw a picture to go with it. Travis chose the story of the Titanic. He wrote that it was a large ship that "ran into an ice cube."

Lost Innocence

The seniors read a story in English literature in which a man was accused of taking a young woman's maidenhead. As a culminating project, groups of students were to present the tale in different media. One group drew a mural. In an opening scene, a woman knelt at a block of wood. Her head was on the ground some distance from her.

"What part of the story is this?" asked Sister Lisbeth, not recalling a woman's execution in the plot.

"Oh, that's where the maiden's head's been taken," explained the artist.

Creativity

Esther was a big-hearted senior who found writing a research paper quite a challenge. Reading her paper, Sister Eileen found a unique feature following the bibliography. Esther had added a page that began, "I found some good quotes that I couldn't get into the paper. Here they are. Love, Esther."

Pizzazz

Sister Kathleen knew that Peggy was creative when the students chose a French version of their names to be used in class. Instead of Marguerite, Peggy had chosen Péguy, for Charles Péguy, the French writer. Later, when it was Péguy's turn to report on the French composer Offenbach, Sister learned of Péguy's organizational skills.

At the end of her report, Péguy walked over to the record player and concluded, "Of course, Offenbach is most noted for this." She dropped the needle on a record. As the loud strains of the cancan began, the entire class of girls stood and danced, heedless of the fact that their room was directly across from the principal's office.

Location Information

Sister Mary Jane was the school librarian. She enlisted a student's help in searching for a book on a bottom shelf. "See if you can find the book 391.2 for me," she said.

The child crouched and looked for a while. Then he glanced up at Sister and asked, "What was that ZIP code again?"

Three Strikes

As an American Literature assignment, the students were to research two Harlem Renaissance persons other than writers. Their choices needed Sister Rose's approval. One group called Sister over and asked if she would approve the artist they had decided on. Their choice was Leonardo da Vinci.

When Sister frowned, the students asked, "What's wrong?"

Sister replied, "Well, first, he's not American; he's Italian. Second, he's the wrong color. Third, it's the wrong renaissance!"

10. Spelling

"Sister, how do you spell *tofer*, like in Christopher?"

Spelling Champ

The primary children were writing stories. Their teacher pointed out to one lad that he had misspelled a word. With supreme confidence, the boy declared, "This is how I spell it!"

How'zat Again?

Sister Regina had told her fifth-graders that if they didn't know how to spell a word, they should let her know. Before long a hand shot up and a boy asked, "How do you spell *mice-well*?"

Puzzled, Sister asked, "Have you heard this word used?"

The boy said, "All the time."

"Give me an example," Sister said.

"It's cheap, so we mice-well buy it."

Wee Spell

The eighth-grade cheerleaders were the idols of the first-graders. During recess, Sister St. Gerard heard the little ones imitating them. The leader directed, "Give me a *B*," and the aspiring cheerleaders shouted, "*B*." The game went on.

"Give me a *Q*."

"*Q*."

"Give me an "*R*."

"*R*."

Finally the leader asked, "What's that spell?" and one tot called out, "I don't know!"

A Budding Novelist

After developing the week's spelling words, an upper-grade teacher told the students to write a short paragraph using five of the words. Ten minutes later the following paragraph was handed in: "In the <u>aisles</u> of the <u>vehicle</u>, we found piles of <u>rhubarb</u>. The <u>colonel</u> asked the <u>shepherds</u> to help him clean it up, but the shepherds had <u>asthma</u>."

College Demons

When Sister Immaculee taught the seventh-graders that *all right* was two words spelled with two *l*'s," she remarked, "This is one of those spelling demons. What's a demon?"

Mike raised his hand and stated, "I know what a demon is. It's the head of a college. My sister teaches at the college in Toledo, and they have one down there."

A Tough Question

Six-year-old Chris came to Sister Marc and asked, "How do you spell *tofer*. Puzzled, Sister asked, "Do you mean *stiffer* or *tougher*?"

"No," Chris said, shaking his head.

"Use it in a sentence," Sister directed, hoping for enlightenment.

Chris replied, "I want to spell *tofer*, like in Christopher."

Heart Disease

Sister Lorica's English class was giving PowerPoint presentations on famous figures from a certain era. She could barely contain her laughter when one student reported that her person died from an erotic aneurysm (instead of an aortic one).

11. Mathematics

"Don't ever throw snowballs around this place. If you do, she makes you put them into sets and subsets."

New Math

When one of Sister Karlene's kindergartners was reciting his facts at home, his mother was shocked to hear him say, "One plus one, the son of a bitch is two. Two plus two, the son of a bitch is four." Mom called Dad over to verify what she was hearing. A phone call to Sister Karlene clarified that she had taught the children: "One plus one, the sum of which is two," and so on.

One Plus One

Plural forms can be tricky. Sister Meribeth was drilling her second-graders on the rules. At one point, she threw in a hard word to stump them. She asked, "What is the plural of *solo*?" Expecting a child to answer "s-o-l-o-s" or "s-o-l-o-e-s," Sister was dumbfounded when a boy called out, "Duet!"

Superstork

A second-grader was elated by the arrival of a new baby sister, the first girl in a family of boys. Sister asked, "How much does she weigh, Tommy?" Without hesitation the young brother replied, "Eight quarts."

Light Dawns

Sister St. Martha taught algebra to gifted students. One Monday morning, however, the students were not paying attention. In frustration, Sister looked around the room and complained, "I might as well be talking to the lights." One punster in the back of the room quipped, "At least they're bright."

Snow Job

A first-grader was caught throwing snowballs. The principal, Sister Jane Therese, issued the punishment. During the noon break, the little boy was to make fifty snowballs and put them in straight lines. After some time, the culprit called Sister over to see his handiwork. Alas, he had arranged the snowballs in a serpentine design.

Sister said, "No, this won't do. Put them in five rows with ten in each row."

After school, Sister overheard the child telling a friend, "Don't ever throw snowballs around this place. If you do, she makes you put them into sets and subsets."

Fighting Unemployment

Sister Lois commented to her primary math students, "I know some of these math problems are difficult, so it's all right if you make a mistake. We learn from our mistakes." Then she jokingly added, "If you don't make any mistakes, I might not have a job."

That evening Justin, an outstanding math student, was doing his math homework under his mother's supervision. She was surprised to find that most of his answers were incorrect.

"Why do you have so many wrong answers?" she asked.

"Because," Justin explained, "if I don't have wrong answers, Sister Lois will lose her job."

Basic Facts

After years of teaching calculus, Sister Patricia was assigned to teach a general math class. On the first day, she instructed the class to take out a sheet of paper. As the students placed sheets of notebook paper on their desks, to her dismay Sister heard a girl in a front seat mutter, "I can never remember which side the holes go on."

"It's going to be a long year," Sister sighed to herself.

Wrong Number?

The principal noticed little Bobby at the pay phone in the hall. "What are you doing, Bobby?" she asked.

"I left my homework at home. I'm trying to call my mother to ask her to bring it," Bobby replied.

He was using a nickel. Not having any success, Bobby complained, "This slot machine is not working right!"

A Love Letter

A friend shared a little boy's letter with Sister Kirene. It read, "Dear Mom, thank you for helping me with my math. Sensually yours."

12. Science

"Sister, there are tears on your forehead."

Rich Soil

In Sister Marie Aquinas' biology class, the freshmen were naming plants that become our food — such as corn, cabbage, peanuts, apples, and tomatoes. Sister knew she was in an inner-city school when one young man in all seriousness proposed adding ground beef to the list.

A Sticky Question

The first-graders were singing a song about a porcupine that no one would dance with. To make sure that the children understood the song, Sister asked, "What does a porcupine have all over him?"

One boy took a stab at the answer. "Porcs?" he asked.

A for Effort

During class, the fourth-graders had time to read books of their choice independently. Sister Helen Louise noticed one girl was engrossed in the book *The Scarlet Letter*. She walked over to the child, intending to explain that her book was more suitable for high school students. The girl looked up guiltily and proved the point by admitting in a whisper, "I know it's a bad book. It's about a girl who had a baby before she was pregnant."

Whew!

During a science lesson, Sister Mary St. Jude told her eighth-graders that if they had questions about the reproductive system, they should ask their parents. That day, after school, one girl who had a brother in the second grade said, "Sister, you should have been at our house last night. My brother Jimmy asked my dad what sex was. Dad sent him to Mom. She sent him back to Dad because Jimmy asked him first."

The girl explained that in the end her dad asked his son, "Why do you want to know?" Jimmy replied, "Because in my wallet there's a card to fill out, and one of the lines says, 'Sex.'"

Modern Cows

The second-graders were learning about farm life. When Sister introduced the concept that cows give us milk, one boy emphatically stated, "I don't drink cow's milk. I drink store's milk."

Loonartunes Maybe

Sister informed her class, "There will be an eclipse of the moon tonight. Make sure you watch it."

"What channel will it be on?" inquired a student.

Underestimating

Sister Regina was carrying on a conversation about dinosaurs with some primary-grade children. She figured that in talking with such little ones, she needed to speak on a level only slightly higher than baby talk. When a lad showed her a model of a particular dinosaur, she asked, "Oooh, do you think he'd eat me?"

"Oh, no," replied the little boy. "He's not carnivorous."

A Sad Story

Sister Mary Ann was reading a story to a group of preschool children. It was a very hot day. Suddenly one youngster observed, "Sister, there are tears on your forehead."

Anatomy 101

One day after lunch, little Ellen objected to praying with all her heart. "We can't pray with all our heart because it's full of food," she said.

"How's that?" asked her baffled teacher.

"Well," Ellen explained, "when your stomach is full, the food drips over into your heart, and how can you pray when your heart's full of food?"

Protector of the Innocent

One day Bobby came to his teacher and said, "Sister, I hurt my back when I was thrown from the merry-go-round."

"How did that happen?" Sister inquired.

"No one was to blame. It was the centrifugal force that threw me off."

Saving Soil

Sister Elizabeth Marie asked her fifth-graders, "What do farmers do to prevent soil erosion?"

One girl explained, "The farmers scrape the good soil off, collect it, and store it in silos until they need it."

Buried Treasure

An inner-city school was given seeds by the city's garden club so that the children could plant flowers and vegetables at home. As the culmination of the project, the school had a garden day. The children could bring in either actual produce or pictures of their garden.

One child, on seeing the carrots that another child had grown, exclaimed, "Oh, I brought in leaves like that, but I didn't know they had carrots at the bottom!"

A Loony Idea

Sister Susan taught astronomy to a group of challenged eighth-graders. One day a student made what might be considered a logical observation. He asked, "When the astronauts went to the moon, it was a full moon, wasn't it? Because they could never land on that little one."

Creationism

Reviewing a science lesson on cells, Sister asked her first-graders, "What are the tiny things we're made of called?"

One girl confidently answered, "Dust."

City Children

The kindergarteners were looking at pictures of farm animals. "What do these animals give us?" Sister Regina asked.

The children quickly identified that hens give us eggs, pigs give us bacon, and so forth. But nobody could name what sheep give us.

Sister explained, "Some people give the sheep a haircut, and the sheep's hair is called wool. Other people make warm sweaters and blankets out of the wool."

A little voice called out, "Are there blue sheeps?"

Another teacher had no better luck with her first-graders. One of them thought wool came from wolves.

City Teacher

It was Sister Joela's first year teaching in a rural school. Several ninth-graders had informed her that because they would be showing animals at the county fair, they wouldn't be in school on Friday. John was not one of these. When he didn't appear in class, Sister asked, "Does anyone know where John is?"

John's friend Kyle said, "At the fair."

"Sure. And what is John showing?" Sister asked skeptically.

With a straight face, Kyle said, "Blue-butt pigs."

"Right. What is he really doing?"

"Sister, he is showing his blue-butt pigs."

After school, Sister and her friends went to the fair. They found John cleaning a pigsty. He looked up, saw Sister, and said, "So, you didn't believe Kyle, did you?"

That day Sister learned that there were blue-butt pigs.

Only Plain White

Sister taught at an elementary school in Washington, DC, attended by children of several races and nationalities. She chuckled when Mr. Bailey told about his son who was in her class. The Baileys had ten children. After another baby was born, Mr. Bailey broke the news to the youngest children that their mommy would be coming home with a new baby.

The boy asked, "Is it another white one?"

The father said, "Yes."

The child's face fell and he complained, "Why can't we have colored babies like other people?"

The Lesson That Backfired

One day the third-graders were to learn in science class that food is fuel and gives us heat energy. According to the teacher manual, this concept could be introduced by having the students breathe on their hands. They would feel warm air. Sister Kirene, a first-year teacher, trustingly directed her class to do this. The children all held their hands in front of their faces and blew. Then Sister asked, "What did you learn?"

One boy candidly answered, "I have bad breath."

An Eye-Opener

One of Sister Claudette's third-graders returned after an absence of several days. "You had pink eye, didn't you?" she said to the boy.

"Oh, no. I had something much worse," he replied, shaking his head.

Surprised, Sister asked, "You did?"

The boy solemnly stated, "I had conjunctivitis."

Spotted Skin

Sister Grace is an Irish sister who has a generous sprinkling of freckles. One day she learned a little more about cultural diversity when a Hispanic student asked with concern, "Do those spots hurt?"

A Word of Caution

Sister Donnalee took her second-graders outdoors for a hike. Coming across milkweed, the children asked what it was. Sister told them and squeezed some milk out.

A little while later, the children told her, "Timmy's crying."

"Why?" Sister asked.

"Because he licked the milk. We told him it's poison, so he's going to get sick."

By the time the students returned to the classroom, Timmy had stopped crying but was still and silent. He looked sick. Sister Donnalee sent him to the principal, who sent him to the school nurse, escorted by Michael, a third-grader. The next day, Timmy was fine.

That morning, Michael, who had been a notorious student in Sister's class the previous year, came to her and said in a serious voice, "I'd like to give you a tip. Don't take your children to dangerous places."

Mad Chicken Disease?

A three-year-old child reported to her teacher that her big brother in the first grade had to stay home.

"Why?" Sister asked.

"Because he has the chicken pops."

13. History and Geography

"Sister, could you show me where 114 Park Hill Road is? That's where I live."

Needed: A Magnifying Glass

In the library, four-year-old Stephen was gazing intently at the world globe. Finally he asked, "Sister Janet, could you show me where 114 Park Hill Road is? That's where I live."

A Living Fossil

A four-year-old girl asked her teacher, "Are you older than my father?"

"Yes," Sister Myra said.

"Are you older than my grandfather?" the child continued.

"Yes," said Sister, who knew the grandfather.

"Then you must be older than the dinosaurs."

A Clever Bluff

In history class, Sister Barbara asked her eighth-graders for the definition of *privateer*. Not knowing the answer, Dan offered, "How about an undercover Mickey Mouse fan?"

Mistaken Identity

Sister Marthe was driving her little nephew around Cleveland. They passed Lake View Cemetery, the site of a large, impressive memorial to President Garfield. "That building is the Garfield Memorial," Sister informed the lad. His eyes grew big and he exclaimed, "All that just for a cat?"

Who's Who?

A young sister was teaching American history to high school juniors. She explained that Thomas Jefferson was influenced by John Locke's theory of social contract, Montesquieu's concept of separation of powers, and the thinking of Jacques Rousseau.

A student in the back of the room asked, "Who?"

Sister repeated, "Jacques Rousseau."

Again, the student asked, "Who?"

So Sister wrote the name on the board. At that, the girl responded, "Oh, I thought you said Jacques Cousteau."

"Who?" Sister asked, since she was unfamiliar with the underwater explorer.

Businessman in the Making

Second-grader Katy, dressed as Thomas Jefferson, reported on this president's life. After her prepared speech, she entertained questions. She called on Kevin.

Kevin asked, "Mr. Jefferson, you said you helped

with the early banking of money in America. Did you bring any to share with us?"

A Capital Answer

The fifth-grade class was practicing the state capitals by playing Traveler. For this game, a child stood beside another child's desk and the two raced to name the state that matched the capital that Sister Regina called out. The first one to give the right answer moved to stand by the next child's desk and continued to play. At one point in the game, Sister said, "Concord."

Instantly, one eager contestant called out, "Grapes!"

Always Be Prepared

In a college class, Sister Frederic taught her students how to read Shakespeare's plays aloud so that as teachers they could present the plays to their classes. One student, Sister Denis, thought, "I don't need to know how to do this. I'll simply play a record for my class."

The day arrived when Sister Denis had to teach *Macbeth* to an English class. She checked out the record from the school library. On the night before the first lesson, she discovered that the record contained only excerpts — and that it was broken into pieces!

Unfazed, Sister called a student who worked at the public library and asked her to bring a recording of *Macbeth* to school. The student did — a recording of Verdi's opera *Macbeth*, in Italian.

Sister Denis and her students read Shakespeare aloud.

That's News to Me

Sister St. Gerard decided to make her third- and fourth-graders more aware of current events. She told them that as homework they were to watch the news on the television with their parents. The next day she asked the class, "What did you learn from the news last night?"

One youngster waved his hand wildly and then shared, "I found out that even in Italy they got teenagers."

Nine Lives?

Sister Mary Jane was the high school librarian. One day during study hall in the library, a boy approached her and asked, "Do you do writing?"

"Yes," Sister said.

"Would you read my composition and tell me what you think?" the student asked.

Sister read his paper on *Macbeth* and chuckled when she came upon a sentence that began, "The first time Banquo was killed...."

Taking a Shot at It

In Sister's fourth-grade class, there was a boy from the Middle East. One day she asked what the Fourth of July was, and he volunteered to answer. The child explained, "In the past they shot cannons. Today we fire crackers."

14. Music

"I'm just warming up for my piano lesson, Sister."

Improvised Band Music

During a science lesson, Sister Marisa's second-graders were given an unusual experiment. Holding one end of a rubber band in their teeth, the children were to stretch it and then pluck it in order to hear various tones. As the children did this, the room was filled with the sound of rubber-band music.

Suddenly, there was an odd "plink." One lad's loose front tooth had shot out onto the floor.

Giving Away the Whole Word

The first-graders were having a music lesson. Tom was asked to identify the kind of musical note Sister was pointing to.

"Tell me the first letter of the name, Sister," he pleaded.

"*W*," answered the teacher. That didn't help. Tom begged to be told another letter.

"*H*," Sister said grudgingly.

This hint shed no light either. After much persuasion, Sister finally revealed the next letter, namely *O*.

"Long or short?" Tom asked.

Piano Exercise

Nhi was a second-grader who spoke Vietnamese at home. One day she came for her piano lesson before Sister Ellen was ready. Sister directed, "Nhi, go to the piano and warm up."

A few moments later Sister looked up and saw Nhi behind the piano doing jumping jacks! The little girl had learned about warm-ups in phys-ed class.

Music Critic

Sister Kathleen was the school's French teacher. One day she taught the first-graders the song "Frère Jacques" and translated the words. A sophisticated little boy commented, "I think that's a pretty stupid song."

Three Italian Trombones?

Sister Ellen asked her music students to name the four adult voice parts. The child who answered got most of them right. She said, "They are soprano, alto, trombone, and bass."

A New Song

Sister explained that there would be a school Mass to celebrate Easter.

"Are we going to sing the Tah-dum again?" a boy inquired.

"Tah-dum? What's Tah-dum?" Sister asked.

"He means the *Te Deum*," a classmate helped out.

Change of Voice

Jimmy was in the choir that sang a special song for the Christmas Midnight Mass. On the first day back at school, he asked his teacher, "Sister, did you hear a squeak during the song? Because I think I squoke."

15. Art

"Sister, I hate to have to tell you this, but
you hung mine upside down."

A Polite Picasso

After a visit to the marsh, Sister Myra's preschoolers
drew pictures of it. Sister displayed the pictures on the
wall. Soon after, a little boy came to her and with sweet
sensitivity said, "I hate to have to tell you this, but my
picture is upside down."

Sister had transposed the blue sky and the blue
water.

A Colorful Question

The first-graders were studying the color wheel. Sister explained, "Black and white aren't really colors. Black is the absence of color. And white is all colors combined."

Immediately, one perplexed child asked, "If black and white aren't colors, then why the heck are they in the crayon box?"

A Wasted Degree

Sister Susanne had a master of fine arts with a major in drawing. Yet as she helped a kindergarten student draw a strawberry, the child looked at her with concern and said, "You're not very good at drawing, are you?"

A Coat of Many Meanings

As an assignment, Sister Lisbeth had the juniors design a coat of arms for themselves. One girl understood the part about drawing symbols to reflect her life, but the basic concept of a coat of arms was foreign to her. She drew her symbols inside the outline of a coat that had numerous arms extending from it.

A Surrogate Mother

The kindergarten teacher saw to it that her children's clothes were protected during art lessons. She explained that they wore aprons so that their mothers wouldn't have to wash paint out of their clothes.

One day, during a messy art lesson, the teacher got paint on her clothes. A little girl commented, "You're your own mudder, aren't you?"

A Trick on the Teacher

Sister Kathleen planned to have her first-graders make papier-mâché heads of what they were going to be for Halloween. She had read that adding grease to white glue makes a better mixture. On the day of the lesson, a teacher aide appeared wearing a beautiful suit and high heels. She helped the children dip the strips of newspaper into the super-gooey mixture and drape them over the balloons.

All was going well until a balloon burst and went flying around the room, hitting the new flashcard chart and leaving a grease mark. Soon other balloons laden with wet strips of newspaper were careening around the room. The balloons were too thin to hold the sopping paper. Other balloons were falling off their cardboard bases onto the carpet. At the end of the day, a scrap of red balloon dangling from the ceiling remained as a reminder of the tragedy. The teacher aide never returned.

Flavored Paper

No elementary-school art class would be complete without manila paper. One day a child volunteered, "Sister, can I pass out the butterscotch paper?"

A Thimple Thuggethion

Sister Marian was conducting a cutting-and-pasting art lesson with her second-graders at the end of the school day. When the bell rang to prepare for dismissal, several children weren't finished with their projects.

Colleen, who was missing two front teeth, came to Sister and said, "Thithter, if you would thtop before the bell ringth, we wouldn't get tho exthited when the bell ringth!" From that day on, Sister never scheduled art as the last lesson of the day.

A Funny Bunny Tale

Sister Suzanne squeezed under the table with the four-year-olds, who were holding the bunny puppets they had made. They were hiding from Mr. McGregor. All of a sudden, one child turned to Sister and remarked, "Know what? I think you're having as much fun as we are!"

16. Home Economics

"Now I just pour the pudding into the
water to cool it off, right, Sister?"

A Flaky Baker

Linda was supposed to bring in cupcakes for her
class as a fund-raiser. Knowing Linda, her classmates
thought she would forget. Linda surprised everyone by
remembering the cupcakes. Not only that. They were
delicious.

Then Linda reestablished her former reputation

as a dingbat. When her friends praised her cupcakes, she explained, "The hardest part was getting the little papers to stick to them."

Chocolate Mix-Up

The freshmen in Sister St. Martha's home economics class were making chocolate pudding, a fairly easy dessert. One girl, however, had let the mixture cook too long, and it was very hot. Sister pushed the faucet over to the girl's side of the sink and told her to fill the sink with cold water to cool off the pudding.

A few seconds later, when Sister glanced back, she saw the girl about to pour the saucepan of pudding into the sink of cold water.

Survival Skills

In science class, when it was time to demonstrate the effect of high and low temperatures on materials, Sister Renetta sent Kevin to the faculty room to fill a beaker with ice cubes. A short while later, he returned minus the ice.

"Sister, I didn't know how to get the ice cubes out of the trays," he explained.

Realizing that Kevin was probably not the only modern ninth-grader who was used to the convenience of ice cubes dropping from a dispenser at home, Sister sent him back for a tray of ice cubes. She then taught a basic home economics lesson: the effect of running warm tap water over frozen water.

17. Physical Education

"AA? Let's see … yes, there was a meeting of the Athletic Association this morning, but that's just for girls."

Tipsy Information

One day Sister Frank, physical education teacher at Notre Dame Academy, was acting as the school receptionist. A man came into the building and asked where the AA meeting was. Thinking of her Athletic Association meeting, Sister immediately responded, "Oh, it was this morning, but it's just for girls." Luckily, a more experienced sister came by and directed the man to the

Alcoholics Anonymous meeting at the church across the street.

Team-Wreck

Josh, a sixth-grader, was bemoaning the fact that his little league football team had won a game 48 to 6. He complained, "It should have been 48 to 0, but a dumb fifth-grader got in my way just as I was about to tackle the scorer."

Sister explained, "But that was what he was supposed to do."

Josh replied, "But the fifth-grader was on my team!"

Delayed Reaction

Sister Constant laid down a firm rule for her young students: If they forgot their gym clothes, they may not have gym. No gym clothes, no gym.

A few days later, when the children were supposed to change into their gym clothes, one boy did not move. He sat there crying, his gym clothes nowhere in sight. When Sister went to the distraught boy, he looked up and said defensively, "I'm not crying because I forgot my gym clothes."

"Oh? Then why are you crying?" Sister asked.

"Because my grandfather died," the tyke replied.

A bit suspicious, Sister questioned, "And when did your grandfather die?"

"Five years ago."

The Importance of Previews

As moderator of the Athletics Association, Sister Mary Marthe planned to show three hundred girls the movie *Fundamentals of Good Bowling* in an activity period. By the scheduled day, the movie still hadn't arrived. But then, that morning, Sister Dina, the school secretary, called Sister and said, "Don't worry. The film's here. I'll have it on the projector all set to go for you."

During the activity period, as students pulled down the black shades in the auditorium, Sister Marthe explained that the movie would teach them basic things that make the difference between a good bowler and a bad one.

She turned on the projector, and a lady in a pink negligee appeared on the screen. The woman asked, "Do you know if you need a two-way stretch girdle, a panty-girdle, or just a garter belt? Do you need a front-laced corset or a back-laced one? Do you wear cup size A, B, or C?"

Instantly Sister Marthe flicked off the projector, while the auditorium rang with peals of laughter. The film, which had been placed in the wrong canister, was entitled *How to Select a Foundation*.

Topsy-Turvy Tommy

Because the physical education teacher was absent, Sister Kirene was asked to take the two classes of first-graders for gym class. That had been her worst subject in school! But she remembered how her gym teacher, Mr. Farms, had taught her class how to stand on their heads by first resting their knees on their bent elbows. So that is what she taught the little ones, quite successfully. For at a parent-conference meeting, Matthew's parents informed her that whenever they wanted to know where their son was, they would look for feet in the air.

18. Teachers

"I was just standing here, and suddenly I got plastered."

Tongue Twisters

One year the students in Sister Kathleen's English classes had particularly unusual names. It required real effort to keep Lavitha, Latonya, and LaRonda straight. In the class were two good-sized girls, one named Basilica and the other, Parthenia. One day, when Parthenia raised her hand, Sister's wires crossed and she called, "Parthenon?"

A Greenhorn

For her first year of teaching, Sister Agnesmarie, a city girl, was assigned to fifth grade in a rural school. During one lesson she explained to her students that food is stored in a silo so that the animals will have food in the winter.

"What do they store in the silo?" asked Sister. Hands flew up.

"All right, Terence, what do they put in the silo?"

"They put fodder up there," Terence answered.

Fodder was not in Sister's vocabulary at that time. "Terence," she said firmly, "are you trying to be funny? We are not talking about your father."

Double-Crossed

Sister Regina Zeleznik once had a student in class who had the same last name as she did. That year Sister's father retired, and she spoke to him on the phone more often than usual. One evening another Sister summoned her to the phone, saying, "It's Mr. Zeleznik."

Using her dad's pet name for her, Sister Regina took the receiver and said cheerfully, "Hello! It's your sweetheart."

Her greeting was met with a very long silence.

A Cover-Up

As the filmstrip began, Sister Barbara Ann realized that she had threaded it the wrong way for her senior class. The reversed words on each frame were illegible. Thinking quickly, Sister explained to the students, "Words sometimes distract us from the visual impact of a filmstrip. We will view this filmstrip with the words blurred so that we can better absorb the message as a whole." With dignity intact, Sister proceeded to show the filmstrip.

First-Day Daze

It was Sister Johnica's first year of teaching. On the first day of school, another Sister walked into her classroom and asked, "Do you have an abacus?"

Sister Johnica replied, "Just a minute. I'll check my attendance book."

The Teacher Who Failed

Sister Maretta, the principal, was hard up for a substitute for the first grade. A former eighth-grade teacher, she gritted her teeth and went in to spend the day in the first grade herself. As the morning dragged on, it became obvious that she was having a difficult time keeping the class occupied with worksheets. One little boy sighed and helpfully suggested, "Why don't we all just go home?" And Sister thought, "My sentiments exactly."

Absent-Minded Professor

During her college economics class, Sister Helen needed her reading glasses to read something to her students. She shuffled through the piles of papers on her desk until the girl in the front seat asked, "Sister, what are you looking for?"

"My glasses," Sister replied.

"You're already wearing them," the girl informed her.

Yes, the glasses were right on Sister's nose.

Double Meaning

Sister Luke, a sweet, elderly nun, was telling her students about how part of a ceiling had fallen the previous day. "I was standing in the classroom, and suddenly I got plastered," she innocently said.

Fresh Information

Sister Karita returned from a trip with students and was asked to park the van back in the garage. "I can do this," she thought. She pulled up to the garage door, pressed the opener remote, and nothing happened. She pressed it repeatedly to no avail.

Assuming that the battery was dead, Sister took the remote into the school and explained the situation. The principal, Sister Joanne, looked at the remote, burst out laughing, and said, "Why, Sister, that's the air freshener!"

Flustered, Sister asked, "Well, how do I get the door open?"

"You walk over to it and pull it up," Sister Joanne said, still laughing.

A Know-Nothing Nun

One of the high school students in study hall approached Sister LeRoy with a question. Sister couldn't answer. The girl returned to her seat. A while later, the girl came to Sister again with another question. Again Sister couldn't answer. Exasperated, the girl exclaimed, "Gee, don't you know geometry either?"

Caught in the Act

Sister Kirene's fifth-floor classroom was next to a few stairs that led to the school roof. One day the principal alerted her that her twelfth-graders were going onto the roof and dropping erasers on the grade school kids below. Later, while Sister was teaching English, out of the corner of her eye she spotted figures going up the steps. She dashed out of the room and up the steps, threw open the door, and scolded, "What do you think you're doing up here?"

Two surprised men explained that they were from

the diocesan facilities services department inspecting the building. They commended the red-faced sister for her diligence.

A Big Compliment

The kindergarteners were allowed to celebrate their birthdays by wearing special clothes to school. On their teacher's birthday, she decided to dress up too. Her efforts were rewarded when one little boy declared in awe, "Oh, Miss Hall, you are so pretty." With emphasis, he repeated, "You are so-o-o pretty." Then to convince her of his utter admiration, he said, "You are as pretty as Miss Piggy."

Cheaper by the Dozen

Sister Christa was in charge of ordering 230 doughnuts for the school's First Friday breakfast. After she phoned in the order, the bakery called back three times to verify the number. How odd, she thought.

On Friday morning not one but two trucks pulled up to the school. They were delivering 230 dozen doughnuts. The children ate as many doughnuts as they could, and families helped out in the crisis by purchasing a dozen or two.

Putting Teachers in Their Places

The students were assigned parking spaces for their cars. One morning a boy came to Sister Allison, the principal, and complained that someone's car was in his space. After some investigation, Sister discovered that the car belonged to a teacher. She called the man to the office and asked what his parking space was. He admitted, "I lost my tag, but I distinctly remember that it said I could park in either 98 or 99."

Sister responded, "That can't be. No one has two

spaces." Then it dawned on her that the tags were good for the years 1998 and 1999. The teacher was promptly reassigned a spot.

Equals

Sister Teresemarie often engaged a high school student named Tom in conversation about theology. He was eager to learn. One day after school, when the boy had finished cleaning the chemistry lab and Sister had finished doing her convent housework, the two met at the incinerator with their respective garbage. Tom immediately greeted her with, "Well, Sister, we meet again, but now on the same level."

Great Expectations

The phone rang and Sister Regina answered.

"I'd like to speak to a teacher," a little voice said.

"This is a teacher," Sister replied.

"Well, could you tell me the name of the third-largest Hawaiian island?"

"No," said Sister.

"Are you a teacher?" the voice asked again.

"Yes," Sister assured the caller.

"Well, what is the name of the third-largest Hawaiian island?" the voice repeated.

"I don't know."

"Is there a real teacher there I could speak to?"

A Slow Student

During indoor recess, the third- and fourth-graders were playing school. Taking part in the game, the teacher, Sister Janet, sat in a child's desk. Adam, who was playing the role of the teacher, came up to her and asked, "And just how many years have you been kept back?"

Cool Compliment

While Sister Doreen was tutoring six-year-old Donald, his gaze kept going off the worksheet and up to her. After having to bring his attention back to the task for the third time, she inquired, "What are you looking at?"

"Your hair," Donald replied.

"What is it with my hair?" Sister asked.

"Well," he said, "it's like gray in the front, and it's black in the back."

"So," she said, "is there something bothering you about that?"

"No, I just think it's cool!"

Lack of Experience

One evening Sister Christa got a phone call from a parent who asked for information about euthanasia. "I'm sorry," Sister replied, "I've only taught youth in America and don't know anything about youth in Asia."

A Human Alarm Clock

At 8:00 a.m., on the first day of school, the convent doorbell rang. When Sister opened the door, she saw a first-grader standing there. He asked, "Is Sister Mary Audrey up yet?"

The Eye of the Beholder

One junior-high boy stared hard at Sister Maurene, the new principal. She looked familiar. Finally, he realized that she had once been his kindergarten teacher. He gasped in amazement and said, "I can't believe that she's gotten so small!"

Caught in the Act

Sister Alice was showing a movie that she had shown in other biology classes that day. Sitting at a table in the back of the room, she thought it was safe to close her eyes and rest. When she opened her eyes, all of the students were gathered around the table, gazing at her. The projector's light bulb had burned out so that, although the movie was still running, the screen was black.

They Try Hard

One of Sister Lisbeth's French classes never reacted to her jokes in French. The students knew they were disappointing her. One day after Sister had told a joke, a girl whipped out a card that said, "Ha, ha," and the class laughed. "Well, I'm glad at least someone got the joke," Sister said.

"Oh, I didn't get the joke," the girl with the card admitted, "but I can tell when you are telling a joke by the change in your voice."

School Daze

On the first day of school, when it was time to go home, a little boy didn't know what bus to take. He came crying to Sister Madelle. She told him, "Go to your teacher, and she'll help you get on the right bus."

The lad looked up at Sister and sobbed, "But Sister, you're my teacher!"

New Job

One year the crop of tomatoes at the rural school was so abundant that the Sisters decided to sell them after school. When parents came to pick up their children, Sister Berchmans, the third-grade teacher, stood in the driveway with some baskets of tomatoes.

A little boy went up to another sister and said, "You know the teacher I had last year? She sells tomatoes now."

Bested by Jesus

One day the religion lesson was moved to after lunch and playground break. Sister Judith's second-graders came into class wound up and not ready to concentrate. She attempted to calm them down by offering the disciples of Jesus as models.

"Boys and girls," she said, "whenever Jesus spoke to people, they all listened to his every word. In fact, the people gave all their attention to Jesus. He was the best teacher ever!"

A hand quickly went up, and a lad stated, "Sister Judith, you're a close second!"

Fancy Footwork

Sister Michael, the principal of the preschool, had hammertoes. One day, when she wore sandals to school, a tyke stared at her feet, fascinated. Then he exclaimed, "Wow! How did you get your toes to do that?"

Puberty?

One day Sister came to school with a cold that left her with a deep, raspy voice. Six-year-old Bryon informed her, "Sister, your voice is changing!"

Telltale Hearts

Sister Lisa was transferred in the middle of the year. The teacher who had been substituting in the fifth-grade class until she arrived did her a great favor. In the back of the room was a bulletin board to welcome Sister. It was full of decorated hearts, each with a student's name.

The teacher aide revealed to Sister Lisa that the

hearts were secretly coded. The gold hearts were the best students. The green ones were the children that had hope. The red hearts were those children who were potential troublemakers. The purple hearts were those Sister would really have to keep an eye on.

Negative Praise

Sister Helen Frances celebrates her name day on October 4, the feast of St. Francis of Assisi. One of her high school students presented her with a card on this day. Touched, Sister opened the card and read, "Sister, to me you betray everything St. Francis stands for. Happy feast day!"

Painted Into a Corner

Margie was painting scenery flats brown for the school play. As she worked, she chatted with Sister Lisbeth. "You know, there are only two teachers who like me, you and Sister Lisa."

With that, Margie turned around and in the process painted a wide swath of brown paint across Sister's middle. "Oops," said Margie. "One Sister who likes me."

Student Vigilante

Every day the primary classes received a grade for their conduct at lunch. When the children were back in class, their teachers wrote a letter on the board: *E* for excellent, *G* for good, and *P* for poor. One day, as the teachers ate in the faculty dining room, they were unusually exuberant. To their surprise, a sheet of yellow primary paper came sailing under the door with a large *P* written on it. The next day the same thing occurred, but this time the paper bore an *E*.

19. Principals

"I'm God. I have to appear in just a minute."

The Prudish Principal

Over the PA system, the principal announced the beginning of the Catholic newspaper drive. The students in the class that sold the most subscriptions would be awarded a bust of Pope St. Pius X. To avoid saying the word *bust*, Sister said that the winning class would receive half a statue.

The priest who was teaching religion heard this announcement and told a student to go and ask Sister which half.

Hi, God!

St. Anselm's Church was in the center of the school. One Saturday morning Sister Annamae, the CCD principal, was walking through the halls when she saw a tot standing in front of the church doors. Knowing that class had already begun, she asked the child, "Now, who are you?"

"I'm God," came the disconcerting answer.

"And what is God doing out here in the hall?" Sister asked.

"I'm waiting. I have to appear," the child replied.

Only then did Sister remember that the first grade was having a pageant that morning.

School for Cooks

On the day before school started, Sister Marcella, the principal, was practicing her announcements for the next morning, unaware that the PA system was actually on. All the teachers who were working in their rooms heard her say, "Today you did not have to wear your uniforms. Tomorrow, however, all boys and girls should wear their school uniforms. On Friday, please bring in Betty Crocker coupons. Remember, tomorrow everyone should wear a Betty Crocker uniform."

A Like Letter

A class from an inner-city school visited a class in a rural school. A few days later Sister Virginia, the principal of the host school, received this note of gratitude: "Dear Sister, I liked your school in the country. I liked the dining room and the gym. I liked playing in the snow. I liked the cows and pigs. I also liked you."

A Secret Life

Little Jamie had frequently come to school with his mother, who worked in the cafeteria. There he often chatted with Sister Jeanne Marie, the principal. Finally, the day came when he entered kindergarten. One day he spotted Sister Jeanne Marie in the principal's office. "What are you doing here?" he asked.

"I'm working," Sister Jeanne Marie answered.

"But why are you in the principal's office?" Jamie asked.

"Because I'm the principal," Sister said.

Shocked, Jamie exclaimed, "You mean all these years I've been talking to the principal?"

The Eraser That Flew

Sister Regina was principal of a one-story school in Virginia. One day a teacher brought a first-grade girl to her and said, "Tell Sister what you did."

The little girl began clapping her hands together rhythmically. She explained, "I was clapping erasers outside, and one of them went on the roof." She continued clapping her hands.

"All by itself?" asked Sister Regina. "Didn't you do something else?"

Still clapping her hands, the little girl replied, "Well, once I went like this," and turned one hand face up.

"Didn't you also go like this?" Sister prompted, making a hurling motion.

A Trick That Fell Flat

On April Fools' Day, four sophomores came to school late and claimed that they had had a flat tire. When the principal inquired, "Where did it happen?"

the girls' shifty eyes clued her in that something was amiss.

"On Green Road," one girl answered.

Handing each girl a slip of paper, Sister directed, "Write down which tire went flat." After the slips were returned, she glanced at them and then said with mock sympathy, "You poor girls, not one but all four tires went flat!"

Twins?

During lunch in the school cafeteria, a small girl revealed to her classmates that her birthday was July 4 and so her family called her a firecracker. The principal overheard this. She whispered in the girl's ear, "I was born on July 4, too."

The child looked up at Sister wide-eyed and asked, "How did you get to be so big so fast?"

Testing the Waters

The kindergarten teacher was not in her classroom, and the children were taking advantage of it. Hearing the commotion, Sister Maurene, the principal, walked to the room and stood in the doorway. In her firmest principal voice she commanded, "Sit down."

One wee girl walked over to her and looking up asked, "Is that as mad as you get?"

20. Supervisors

"But you couldn't ride one now, because you'd squash the poor pony."

First Impression

Several months into the new school year, it was announced that the school supervisor would visit. She would observe a class in the first grade. Sister Madelle, the first-grade teacher, planned a terrific lesson. She intended to impress the supervisor, especially by her skillful use of audiovisuals.

The day of the visit arrived. The supervisor sat in the

back of the classroom. The children were well behaved. Sister flicked on the overhead projector, and a picture appeared on the screen. The whole class gasped in awe and said, "Oooh!" making it quite clear that Sister had never used the overhead projector before.

Pest Control

Sister Rita Mary was supervising at a school in Florida. The children in one class were singing a song for her. Suddenly, a young boy sprang from his place, ran to the front of the room, and stomped on a cockroach. Triumphantly he announced, "Got him! That's three today."

Perspective

Sister Patrice was a first-year teacher being supervised for the first time. During the phonics lesson, she was showing flashcards to her first-graders. They were to read each word and use it in a sentence. Everything was going along fine until it came to the card that showed "p-o-s" for the short "o" sound. Sister held up the card, and a child read, "Pos."

Sister asked, "Can you use it in a sentence?"

The child replied, "We had pos for dinner."

Hoping to clarify the meaning of the word, Sister asked for another sentence. A child obliged and said, "Did you see that pos go down the street?"

"Can we have another sentence?" Sister asked.

Yet another child answered, "My mother bought a new pos."

Then smiling, the supervisor suggested, "Sister, try turning the card around."

Sister turned the card around. "Pos" became "sod."

A Pony Tale

The superintendent of schools was visiting the school. He stopped in the first-grade classroom, where the children were reading a story about a pony. Sister Roseann asked the children if they thought Monsignor had ever ridden on a pony. The children answered, "No, Sister."

But Monsignor interjected, "I did, when I was a little boy."

One fellow, sizing up the priest's robust form, remarked, "But you couldn't ride one now, because you'd squash the poor pony."

Monsignor laughed heartily, to Sister's relief.

An Encouraging Word

Sister Mary Jane, a school supervisor, observed a class of third-graders. Afterwards, she congratulated them: "Boys and girls, keep up the good work."

Spontaneously, they answered in chorus, "You too, Sister!"

Stomach Problem

The school psychologist sat in Sister Catherine's first-grade classroom to observe a girl named Sue. During the course of the lesson, Billy started crying. The psychologist took him out into the hall.

When Sister had a chance to speak to the psychologist, she discovered that he had been watching the wrong Sue.

"And what's the matter with Billy?" she asked.

"Oh, he was just hungry," the man replied.

MTV Forerunner?

The supervisor was observing Sister Judellen teach high school English. Sister had never been observed before and was a nervous wreck. She managed to control her shaking hands and trembling voice quite well. But Sister's state of mind was revealed when it was time to play a music selection. She carried the record, not to the record player, but to the overhead projector and set it on the glass.

Moral Support

The new diocesan social studies curriculum was implemented in Sister Rita Mary's classroom. On the day diocesan officials were coming to observe the children, one little girl asked Sister, "What do we do if we get nervous?"

Sister replied, "Look at me and I'll smile at you. Then you won't be nervous."

Promptly, another girl reassured Sister, "And when you get nervous, Sister, just look at me, and I'll smile at you."

Caught in the Act

Sister Mary Jane, a diocesan supervisor, visited the Montessori school. She noticed a sign that read, "Please do not talk to the children." Sister went about quietly, watching the youngsters doing their jobs. One very small girl followed her for a while and then whispered out of the side of her mouth, "What is your name?"

Not exactly knowing what to do, Sister whispered back, "Sister Mary Jane."

The little one kept following and after some moments whispered, "What are you doing here?"

Sister looked at her and whispered, "I'm here to see if you are doing your work."

Quick as a flash, the tot was back at her tiny table, intent on her very important task.

Mixed Numbers

As a student teacher, Sister Lisa was under the impression that she was not supposed to hold her lesson plans as she taught. One day the college supervisor was to observe her junior-high math class. To prepare for the math problems that the students would work at the board, Sister carefully wrote the answers on the palm of her hand. Her nerves, however, were her undoing.

A group of students went to the board and worked the first problem. Sister glanced at her hand for the answer. To her dismay, her hands were sweating so much that the numbers had all run together. To check the students' answers, she then depended on the answers of the majority.

21. Students

"I'm going to beat you, babe!"

Consumer Children

The kindergarten teacher gave her class a worksheet on the letter *b*. She directed them to put a check in front of each word that began with *b*. "Do you understand the directions?" she asked. "Yes," they said. However, as the teacher walked around the class, she found that instead of a check mark, some children were marking the *b* words by drawing a horizontal box with scribbles and lines inside.

What was it? A bank check, of course.

Ours Is Not to Question Why

Sister Kathleen showed the movie *Macbeth* to her seniors. At the end, when the lights were turned on, she saw that the entire film had not run onto the second reel but onto the floor in a pile. There was a boy seated on either side of the projector.

"Why didn't you tell me this was happening?" Sister asked the boys.

"We thought that's the way you wanted it," they replied.

Missing the Point

The second-grader came up to Sister Sharon's desk and said, "I have to go the bathroom."

Sister corrected him in a whisper, "May I please go to the bathroom."

"Do you have to go too?" he asked.

A Wrong Answer

"How old are you?" a primary-grade child asked Sister Marie Helene.

Instead of giving away her true age, thirty-four, Sister gave her stock answer to this question: "One hundred and thirteen." Then she asked, "How old did you think I was?"

"Seventy," came the answer.

"Pray that you're never in my class," Sister advised.

Checkmate

Sister Margaret had once been a high school principal and a school supervisor. As she neared retirement, she enjoyed working with young children at a parish grade school. Any kindergartener who wished to join the school chess club first had to beat Sister at checkers.

One day a little lad who longed to play chess sat down across from Sister at the checkerboard and challenged, "I'm going to beat you, babe!"

And he did.

Extra Credit for the Teacher

The principal was visiting the classrooms of new teachers. In one room the students were unusually alert and responsive. Before leaving, the principal congratulated the students on their interest and active participation. One member of the class explained, "Sister tried especially hard today to make the class interesting."

A Kind Assist

Sister had told her first-graders a story about a coming feast day. Later, intending to review the lesson, she asked if anyone wanted to help her tell the story. Alphonse, the tallest boy in the room, raised his hand and shuffled up to the front from the last row. He stood in front of the teacher's desk, turned to Sister, and said, "I'd like to help you, Sister. Where are you stuck?"

Innocent Victim

Allen was a notorious first-grader. Even the local police knew him. One day he came to school wearing a hat pulled down over his ears. He kept the hat on during class. On the playground at recess time, Sister asked, "Allen, why are you wearing that hat?"

"Because," said Allen.

"Would you take it off for me?" asked Sister.

"Well, OK," Allen grudgingly replied. He took off the hat, saying, "Those electric razors really go fast." Down the middle of his scalp was a bare strip. Allen explained, "I was in the bathroom, and the razor fell on my head."

Self-Defense

At the Montessori school, a three-year-old was having difficulty buttoning his coat. Sister Doloretta said to an older child, "Would you please help that little boy?"

Offended, the little boy stretched to his maximum height, thrust both hands in his pockets, and declared, "I am a *big* boy."

Quickly, Sister amended her request to, "Will the bigger boy please help the big boy with his coat?"

She was rewarded with a smile on the face of the big boy.

Surprise Parties

While checking the children's records, Sister asked Kim when his birthday was. He was perplexed for a few seconds but then recovered his composure and replied, "Oh, Sister, I really don't know. It always comes as a surprise to me."

A Burning Question

During a homily at Mass at the sisters' convent, the priest told of his experience teaching a class on the Eucharist to second-graders. During the twenty-minute lesson, he drew on his knowledge of pedagogy and used media. He thought he had done quite well. Then at the end of the lesson, Father asked if there were any questions. A boy's hand shot up in the air.

"Yes?"

"At what age did you start losing your hair?"

"Oh, about your age."

Drill Resistant

During Fire Prevention Week, the school had a number of fire drills — too many for Mickey, a sixth-grader. He was weary of hurrying outside every time the fire bell rang. When the bell sounded yet again, Mickey requested, "Sister, just make like I'm non-burnable for this next one, okay?"

A Simple Solution

A little boy with the last name of Butts was constantly being teased by his classmates. One day he came home from school and begged his mother, "Mom, can I change my last name to something simpler — like Rodriguez?"

The Birds and the Bees

Little Viola's eyes sparkled as she skipped into the classroom one morning, eager to tell Sister the wonderful news.

"Sister," she crowed, "Mommy laid a baby last night!"

Proposed Promotion

Alex was an unusually bright second-grader. One day after Alex gave a correct answer, Jacob, a classmate, commented, "Alex should be an adult. He knows so much."

A Backhanded Compliment

At the end of the school year, the students wrote thank-you letters to the bishop, who came for school Masses. One child commented on the bishop's homilies. He wrote, "I like when you talk. I especially like the story about the cracked pot. You told it three times."

22. Parents

"Mommy said I could bring some pennies, but don't let the baby come to our house."

Rose-Colored Glasses

The preschoolers were preparing for a Mother's Day prayer service. Sister Rita asked them to think of one thing that made their mother special and to draw a picture to go with it. Sister could not help laughing when one three-year-old held up her picture and proclaimed, "My mother is special because she feeds ants with spray!"

A Cushy Job

Two little ones were discussing their fathers' jobs. One boy said, "My dad sells shoes. What does your dad do?"

The other boy replied, "He's a CPA."

"Oh," said the first child. After a long pause, he asked, "What does he do?"

A little louder, the other boy said, "He's a CPA."

"But what does he do?" repeated the first persistent boy.

With exasperation, the interrogated child shouted, "He doesn't do anything! He's a CPA!"

A Roundabout

In the church parking lot, Sister Kathleen encountered the mother of a former student. "How is Maryann doing?" Sister asked, recalling that this girl was far from a star pupil.

The mother beamed and gushed, "Maryann is doing great. You wouldn't recognize her. She's turned her life around three hundred and sixty degrees!"

The Patience of a Saint

Two weeks before the feast of All Saints, the children at school were given a set of fifty riddles about saints to solve with their families. One father who was a college history professor was determined that his family would be the first to turn in the completed page. The next morning he told his college students, "If I'm a little incoherent today, please excuse me. I was up until 3:00 in the morning doing my children's homework. Now tell me, who is the patron saint of hat makers?"

(In case you're wondering, there are several, including Barbara, Clement, James the Lesser, Michael the Archangel, Philip the Apostle, and Severus of Avranches.)

Removing Old Leaves

For open house, the third-graders had placed booklets of their work on their desks for their parents to see. Jimmy had prudently removed his papers that weren't very good. His mother, however, noticed that his booklet was much smaller than the other children's. When she asked him about it, Jimmy explained the missing papers: "I did those before my improvement."

The Whole Story

On Tuesday, Sister Mary Elizabeth asked first-grader Ann why she wasn't in school the previous day. "Well, we had a big party with all my aunts and uncles, and no one wanted to get up the next day."

Ann handed Sister her absentee note. It read, "Please excuse Ann for being absent due to a lack of transportation."

Relief

The junior-high students and their parents attended an evening session on sex education presented by a doctor and a nurse. At the conclusion, the presenters encouraged the students to ask their parents any questions they might have.

Afterwards, one father and son were driving home alone when the son said, "Dad, I was wondering ... "

Dad's heart began racing; his knuckles turned white on the steering wheel. What was his son going to ask? How would he answer?

Then the boy continued, "When do you think my voice will change?"

SOS

One elementary-school newspaper had a "Dear Jack and Jill" column in which younger children requested information or advice from the eighth-graders. One child wrote, "Dear Jack and Jill: How do you get grass stains out of your pant knees? Please help quick before my mother finds them." The note was signed, "Desperate."

Why Parents Get Gray

An altar boy was needed for the next morning's Mass. Sister Paula decided to call Johnny and ask him to serve. When the phone rang, another boy answered. Sister asked, "May I please speak to Johnny?"

Over the phone she heard the boy yell, "Hey, Johnny! Some foxy lady wants you on the phone."

No Room for One More

The first-graders had heard about the poor pagan babies in mission lands and how money could be donated to help them. The next day Marvin proudly came to Sister with a fistful of pennies. He declared, "Mommy said I could bring some pennies, but don't let the baby come to our house."

Double Dose of Charm

The high school invited a woman to speak to the girls about etiquette. Each student was asked to pay $2.50 for the special class. In Sister Kevin's homeroom, all the girls had paid except Vicky. Finally, one morning Vicky entered the room, walked up to Sister's desk and slapped down a five-dollar bill.

"But the class only costs two-fifty," Sister said.

"My father said to take it twice," Vicky replied.

Misplaced Sympathy

On Grandparents' Day, two first-graders were poring over some old photos their grandparents had brought to school. One child commented, "Poor Grandma and Grandpa. They didn't see in color when they were kids." The other tyke added, "I feel so sorry for them."

Overhearing the children, Sister Suzanne quickly informed them, "They did see in color. It was the old cameras that didn't see in color."

Greatly relieved, one child exclaimed, "Oh, that's sooo good to know!"

23. Sisterly Things

"I never saw a real witch before!"

Besting God

One of Sister Myra's preschoolers announced to her, "When I grow up, I'm going to marry you."

Showing the child the plain silver band on her ring finger, Sister said, "Your mother has a wedding ring like this. What does it mean?"

"That she belongs to my dad," the little boy answered.

"My ring means that I belong to God," Sister explained.

Undaunted, the boy replied, "Well, I would get you one with a stone."

On a Pedestal

When the sisters opened their first school in Memphis, the children were very curious about them. One summer day a group of ragamuffins rang the convent doorbell to meet some of the unfamiliar creatures in the long black robes. As they conversed with the sister who answered the door, one child declared, "We saw your statue in church this morning."

A Fond Farewell

On the last day of school, one child's parting words left Sister laughing. The tot said, "I love hugging you. You're squishy, just like my grandma."

The Name Game

In the past, a Sister's real name, as opposed to her religious name, was always a challenging mystery. One seventh-grade teacher was approached by a student whose cousin knew Sister's uncle's brother-in-law, who worked with the cousin's great aunt.

"Your last name's Maver, isn't it?" the student asked.

"Yes," Sister conceded.

"Aha!" the triumphant boy responded. "Now I only have to figure out your first name."

A Logical Conclusion

A new modular unit for special classes was stationed close to the school. A child seeing it for the first time remarked to a friend, "And here's the sisters' new camper."

The Silencer

The third-graders were on a bus on their way to a local water show. As they rode along, the excited children grew noisier and noisier. Danny was seated near Sister. Suddenly, he turned to Sister, pointed to her veil, and exclaimed, "O boy, Sister! I bet you're glad you have that thing on your head so you can't hear all the noise in this bus!"

And Her Patron Saint Is …

On the first day of school, Sister Mary Gerard always introduced herself and printed her name on the board. One year she told her new students her name but forgot to write it. The following day a mother came to the classroom. She said to Sister, "I just had to come and find out if my son's teacher this year was really Sister Mary Giraffe."

God, the Employer

At the end of the day at Montessori school, one three-year-old asked Sister Doloretta, "Why do you wear that uniform?"

"Because I work for God," Sister explained. "I teach you, and help others, and pray for all the people in the world."

The boy shook his blond head and repeated, "You work for God," as though he couldn't quite take it in.

As he left the building, he was heard confiding to his mother this surprising new thought: "Sister works for God."

Mistaken Identity

At the school where Sister Jean was principal, the first-graders were told the story of the foundress of the Sisters of Notre Dame. In going over the facts, their teacher, Mrs. Manti, wanted to review that Notre Dame means "Our Lady," a title of Mary, Mother of God. She asked, "Who are the Sisters of Notre Dame named after?"

One child responded, "Our Lady."

Mrs. Manti asked, "And who is Our Lady?"

A little girl raised her hand and said, "Sister Jean!"

A Heavenly Teacher

Sister Mary Jo tried to get her second-graders to imagine what heaven was like. There wasn't much of a response. Finally, a little boy in the back raised his hand and suggested, "Aw, Sister. You've been there. Why don't you just tell us about it?"

A Winner

Notre Dame Elementary School is located in the sisters' provincial house. The same large building houses the faculty, sisters in administration, and the sick sisters. Behind the building is the sisters' cemetery.

One year, to celebrate Catholic Schools Week, an essay contest was held. Students were to write on the topic "What makes my school special." An entry from a fifth-grader at Notre Dame began, "In our school we bury the dead teachers in the field behind the gym."

Needless to say, this entry did not make it to the finals.

Rechristened

Sister Mary St. Hugh's unfamiliar name has been garbled by many a first-grader. Once a little girl went home on the first day of school and announced to her family that her teacher was Sister Mary Who. However, Sister prefers her frequent misnomer, Sister Mary Hug.

A First-Rate Audience

The high school production of *Sound of Music* was being performed for an audience of sisters only. The actors were pleased with the appreciative responses they were getting. When the play ended, one girl announced from the light loft, "Well, they won by thirty points."

"Thirty points for what?" asked Sister Lisbeth, the director.

The student explained, "The sisters laughed forty-five times. That gives them thirty points over any audience so far."

A VIP

The Notre Dame Sisters' superior general, who lived in Rome, was coming to visit the school. All the children had been prepared for her visit. Kevin, a kindergartener, conveyed the news to his parents by translating it into kindergartenerspeak. He announced, "Tomorrow the queen of the sisters is coming to visit."

A Super-Sleek Coiffure

Sister Jesse, in her black habit, was sitting in church off to the side with her first-graders. They were waiting for Mass to begin. One of her little girls came meandering down the middle aisle, searching for her class and looking very lost. Trying to help, a teacher asked her, "Who is your teacher?" The girl answered, "The one with the long, black hair."

A Postulant Defined

In former days, many girls entered the convent directly after high school. These girls, called postulants, usually attended college. However, Nancy, who entered at an older age and was a certified teacher, was assigned to teach. She wore the postulant's garb: a black blouse and cape and a black skirt.

Shortly after school began, one of Nancy's fifth-graders was overheard explaining to a friend, "My teacher is half a sister and half a lady, but every inch a teacher."

Teacher's Pet?

Exasperated by her students' behavior, Sister exclaimed, "I'm going to teach another grade." One student who was fond of her teacher declared, "If you go, I go."

Bilocation

A class of second-graders listened to a prerecorded radio math program conducted by Sister Mary Stanislas, while Sister herself observed in their classroom. After Sister left the room, a little boy asked his teacher, "Is Sister a miracle Sister?"

"Why? What do you mean, Scott?" his puzzled teacher asked.

"She must be pretty good if she can be on the radio and in our room at the same time," the lad explained.

Saint Sister

A curious fifth-grader asked her teacher, "Sister, what was your name before you were canonized?"

Anything for an Arby's

On the way home, Sister Sebastien stopped at Arby's for a sandwich and a shake. As she waited, the man behind the counter said, "Your food's been paid for."

"By whom?" Sister asked.

The young man nodded at a gentleman in a car at

the drive-through window who was grinning at Sister. She waved her thanks.

The next day, Sister was telling her first-graders about God's goodness. She gave the example of the man's goodness to her. One child asked, "Did you have your hat on?"

"Yes," Sister replied, "I always wear my veil."

Then, very seriously, Michael stated, "Tonight I'm going to pray to God to change me into a girl so that I can become a nun like you."

A John Hancock

At one high school, most of the teachers were Sisters of Notre Dame, who put the initials SND after their names. One day a student handed in a paper with an SND after his name. Knowing that their religious community had not accepted any male members yet, the principal asked the boy about the SND after his name. He explained, "That means signed. I signed it. See."

Mistaken Identity

Sister Joanmarie, a high school teacher, was on a city bus, sitting innocently in the center of the last seat. The bus stopped, and a mom and a little girl boarded. The child saw Sister and, screaming, ran down the aisle toward her. Throwing her arms around Sister, she said, "I never saw a real witch before!"

Wishful Thinking

Second-grade Corey had the custom of hugging Sister Sebastien in the cafeteria every day at lunch. One day he remarked, "I wish you were younger so my arms could go all the way around you." Sister mused that not youth but Slimfast would be the solution.

The Pope's Personal Friend

The morning after it was announced that Pope Francis was elected, a child came running into Sister Frances Marie's homeroom and said, "Sister, aren't you happy that the pope took his name after you?"

24. Discipline

"I have restlessness inside me. It's in my blood."

A Good Excuse

One rambunctious first-grader was sent to the principal because he disturbed the other children. He explained to Sister why he was there: "I have restlessness inside me. It's in my blood."

Getting Attention

Sister Konrad was scolding an incorrigible eighth-grade boy at length. The boy stood staring at her. She thought, "Good. He's finally listening. Maybe this time my words will have an effect."

She continued to scold, while the boy stood perfectly still, transfixed, staring at her. Finally, when she took a breath, he said, "Sister, there's a bug crawling in and out of your veil."

Uncertain Fate

A second-grader was overheard warning some troublesome companions, "If you don't behave, you will be excelled."

Diagnosis

One lad found it hard to stay seated at his desk and would often wander around the classroom. Finally, one of his peers rebuked him: "You must be allergic to your desk."

The Student Prophet

Joey, a seventh-grade Parish School of Religion student, was very talkative. One day he tried hard to get Sister Josetta Marie's attention. Finally, she gave in and said, "Yes, Joey, what is it?"

He said, "Sister, when you die, you'll go straight to heaven."

"Why?" Sister asked.

"Because you're patient with me."

Sister answered, "Joey, put that in writing. I may need it."

See No Evil

A first-year teacher was asked to supervise the seventh- and eighth-grade boys while their teachers were meeting separately with the girls. She was instructed to watch the boys carefully. When the teachers returned, the first-year teacher happily reported that the boys had worked diligently and had not tried a thing.

The eighth-grade teacher's delight turned to dismay a few minutes later when she walked to the back of the room and found the girls' purses in a huge pile where the boys had deposited them after passing them around the room.

Breakfast of Losers

Sister Mary Dolores taught high school chemistry. Although barely five feet tall, she rarely had discipline problems. One day, however, she had to reprimand a hefty, six-foot boy. He retorted, "You know, I eat three of you for breakfast!"

The Root of All Evil

Sister Donnalynn had to scold her first-graders for misbehaving. She suggested that maybe it was the result of taking religion class so late that day. Ten minutes before dismissal, the principal walked into the room and complimented the still-repentant children on being so good at the end of the day. Surprised, one boy raised his hand and exclaimed, "What! We had a miserable day. We didn't put God first."

An Epidemic

A first-year teacher gave her students instructions for an art project. While they worked, she became engrossed in correcting papers at her desk. Time passed. When Sister finally looked up at the class, all the children had green mustaches and beards.

Foiled Again

Sister Christian had tried everything to tame Tom, a wild redheaded sixth-grader, with no results. As a last resort, she taped a green scapular under his desk. This "badge of the Immaculate Heart of Mary" is believed to be a source of great favors when used with faith.

Sister taught a Parish School of Religion (PSR) class in the same room. One Saturday she hid holy cards in the room and sent her PSR students on a treasure hunt looking for them. The next Monday, Sister noticed that a few holy cards were still hidden, so she let her sixth-graders hunt for them. All of a sudden, Tom called out triumphantly, "Look what I found."

He was holding up the green scapular!

Second Thoughts

One morning Jimmy presented his teacher, Sister Marcelita, with a shiny red apple. She set it on her desk. During the day, Jimmy misbehaved and Sister had to discipline the little boy. After the children had gone home for the day, Sister noticed that the apple was missing.

A Diapered Delinquent

Mrs. C's two girls were well behaved in school. Sister was warned, though, to get ready for Andrew, who, at eleven months, was a handful. At Sunday Mass, during the homily, Mrs. C set Andrew on the floor, where he played contentedly with her shoe and the kneeler. She turned her attention to the priest.

When the homily was over, she glanced down, and to her horror Andrew was gone. She scoured the congregation with her eyes, trying to detect any unusual responses. No clue. She looked down once more, and there was Andrew … holding a red high-heeled shoe.

At Communion time, Mrs. C watched to see which woman wobbled up the aisle. She spotted the victim, offered her apologies, and returned the shoe.

The Downfall

One winter day, when Sister Julie Rose had playground supervision during recess, the children invented a new game. They were having a great deal of fun falling into the snow on purpose. To prevent injuries and soaking-wet clothes, Sister decreed, "The next one who falls into the snow has to go inside."

She stepped back, slipped, and fell into the snow. She went inside.

Permanent Bankruptcy

Seven-year-old Justin found it difficult to return library books on time. His fines accumulated until one day he owed a dollar. At the end of the school day, his teacher reminded him to bring in money to pay the fine. In all seriousness, a dejected Justin lamented, "Now I won't be able to buy my new car when I'm sixteen."

A Bunch of Baloney

One first-grader never got his papers finished. Exasperated, the teacher took him to Sister Jane Therese, the principal, and explained the problem. Sister Jane Therese directed the boy, "Bring your lunch here to the office. You may not go to lunch until you finish your work."

When the boy returned, he was put, crying, into a room to do his task. After a short time, the door opened, and a wee voice inquired, "How long does it take for baloney sandwiches to spoil?"

"Oh, years and years," Sister replied.

The door closed again, and five minutes later the papers were finished.

Just Obeying Orders

During indoor recess, Dane and a classmate were racing their Matchbox cars on the windowsill, dangerously close to the classroom plants growing there. When Sister noticed what the two boys were doing, she called, "Dane, watch those plants!"

Shortly after, Sister saw that Dane was no longer playing but just sitting and staring. "What are you doing?" she asked.

In all innocence the lad replied, "I'm watching the plants like you said."

Poor Excuse

The snacks were being cleared at the after-school session when Johnny came to Sister Rita and asked for some.

"Where were you before?" Sister asked.

"In the bathroom," Johnny replied.

"The whole time?" Sister asked.

"Yes, it takes me a long time."

"Most people don't need such a long time," Sister countered. "Maybe you'd better see a doctor. How long has this been going on?

"Oh, about ten years," responded the eight-year-old boy.

Tough Love

Sister Josetta Marie had enough of one rambunctious second-grader in PSR class.

"Go to the principal," she told him.

"But I love you," the tyke replied.

"I love you too. But go to the principal."

An Eye for an Eye

A second-grader was sent to Sister Maurene, the principal, for hitting another child on the head with a book. Since she was in the midst of handling another situation, Sister told the culprit, "Just stand there and think about how you should be punished."

After a while, Sister returned and asked the boy, "Well, how should you be punished?"

The lad, who knew something of justice, woefully replied, "Someone should hit me on the head with a book."

A Grim Job

Sister Marc teaches her kindergarteners to put all their things away when they are finished with their work. One day Tina left her table a mess. Sister called her back and said, "Tina, throw the scraps into the wastebasket, clean up the floor, and put your crayons and scissors away."

Overwhelmed by all this, Tina remarked, "You remind me of Cinderella's stepmother."

Repeat Performance

One school has the rule that at noon no one may go into the building. The exception is if someone is hurt on the playground. One day a little girl entered the school, asking to see the school nurse. The child was sent back outside because her wound wasn't serious.

Shortly after, the school secretary saw the girl at the door again with a friend. She asked, "What is it now?"

Matter-of-factly the friend replied, "She fell once and her teacher sent her outside, so she fell again."

Service with a Smile

Sister Maurene was dismayed when she saw the mess inside one student's desk. She wrote a note and set it on his desk. The note read, "Your desk looks like a branch of the city dump." The boy did manage to clean his desk. That night Sister found her note replaced on the desk's lid. Scrawled under her words she saw "It's the main office."

Bad Luck

The children were engrossed in a board game in which tokens could be moved according to the number shown on a rolled die. Suddenly, children at one table called out, "Sister, he's cheating! He rolled the die three times in a row. He won't give anybody else a turn."

"Well, I couldn't help it," the boy explained. "It kept coming up one."

The Writing on the Wall

Sister Kevin was the assistant principal at a high school. One day she made a comment, and a surprised student asked, "How did you know that?"

"I read it in the graffiti on the wall in the boys' lavatory," Sister explained.

At the end of the next school day, Sister was closing up the building and checked the boys' lavatory as usual. When she pushed upon the door of one stall, she found new words on the wall: "Hi, Sister Kevin!"

A Frightening Zoo

Eighth-grade teacher Sister Michael was also the school principal. One day a certain misbehaving young student was sent to her yet again. The lad walked into the classroom where Sister had warned the eighth-graders not to laugh.

Sister stood the troublemaker in the front of the room and pointed to a cabinet in the back. "See that cabinet," she said to the little imp. "Inside of it are a hypotenuse, a quadrilateral, and a rhomboid. If you are sent here one more time, I will let them out."

The child's eyes grew wide. He never had to be sent to the principal again.

Football Brawl

Too often after football games, the boys ended up fighting. The principal gave them a talking to. "Charity is more important than sports," she said. "If you can't be good sports, there will be no more games."

Apparently, Sister's talk did not work. After the next game, there was another fight. Sternly, Sister began to scold the boys. Then one of them spoke up, "It wasn't us, Sister, honest. It was our parents."

A Little Cheater

The kindergarteners were playing a game that involved rolling a die to determine how many spaces to move. One youngster was determined to win. He carefully cupped the die in both hands, shook it vigorously, and put his eye to a small space between his fingers. Then glancing around furtively, he announced, "It's a 6."

25. Homework, Tests, and Grades

"That hammering noise those men are making is disturbing my brain."

A Goblin Who Reads

Whenever something odd occurred in the class-room, such as a door blowing shut unexpectedly, Sister would comment to her young students, "A goblin must have done it."

One day a concerned father called Sister. He asked, "I want to know why a goblin has been taking my son's phonics book so he can't do his homework."

Spelling Ability

When one first-grade teacher had to give her children an ability test, she thought she'd use psychology to prevent nervousness and fear. She told the children they were going to have a wonderful time with games and puzzles. Suddenly, loud and clear, came an emphatic voice: "This is a test, Sister. It says right here, t-e-s-t. That spells 'test.'"

Boy at Work

Workers were installing a gas line outside while the first-graders were taking a math quiz. One distressed lad finally looked up at his teacher and said, "That hammering noise those men are making is disturbing my brain."

A Quick Finish

As Sister Berneta corrected her freshmen's theology tests, she found one where the reverse side had not even been started. She called the girl whose paper it was to her desk and asked, "Why didn't you do the back?"

Looking startled, the girl replied, "Back? But Sister, at the bottom of the page, it said 'Over.'"

A Definition of *Matching*

A vocabulary test required the students to match the words at the top with their definitions. While correcting the papers, Sister was surprised to see one so covered with meandering lines that it looked like a map. Instead of writing the letters of the words after the definitions, the creative child had drawn lines from the definitions to the words.

Fake Punches

At Regina High School, the exams were usually multiple-choice questions, for which the students indicated their answers by coloring over the letters *a*, *b*, *c*, or *d*. To correct the exams easily, teachers made a cover sheet with holes punched out over the right answers.

Before a chemistry exam, Sister Bernette played a review game with her students. She promised them that the one who had the highest score in the game would receive the answers to the exam as a prize. True to her word, at the end of the game she handed the winning girl an envelope. In it were all the circles that had been punched out from the cover sheet, each with an *a*, *b*, *c*, or *d*.

Free A's

Sister Nancy tried in vain to get her physics students to read the bulletin boards that she so carefully changed periodically. On the day of the final exam, she announced to her class, "I'm sure you'll have no problem with this exam. All week long it's been posted on the bulletin board with the answers."

The class screamed.

A Low Goal

On John's report card for the first semester, Sister Claude, his history teacher, wrote a *D* and added the comment, "John will have to try hard to maintain this grade." When she reviewed the grades, she realized that she had made a mistake. John actually was failing the course. Relieved to have discovered the error before the cards were sent home, Sister erased the *D* and wrote in an *F*. Unfortunately, she neglected to change the comment.

Healthy Self-Esteem

One precocious four-year-old asked his teacher to raise his A to an A-plus. He explained, "Because that's how good I am!"

An Intellectual's Threat

Sister Anne, the principal, explained over the PA system, "Words can hurt as much as hitting or guns. No one should be calling names. No one should be threatening. No one should be verbally abusive in any way. If anyone is that way, children should let their teacher know so that the matter can be talked about before it gets out of hand."

That afternoon two fifth-grade boys came to Sister Anne. One boy said, "Sister, we don't want to get him into trouble, but we got a threatening note from Michael." Michael was an excellent student who once wrote a paper on photosynthesis simply because he was interested in it.

"You better show me the note," Sister said. One boy handed her a sheet of notebook paper. On it she read, "You better keep an eye on your extra credit."

When Sister got the boys together, she discovered that Michael didn't like the other boys calling him short. To control them, he threatened what he held of value — extra credit.

A Loozing Battle

Grammar and Composition was a new elective course for juniors and seniors. At the end of the first quarter, Sister asked the class to evaluate themselves. One student wrote, "I think I deserve an A cause I didn't no nothing when I started the course." Another student wrote, "I really learned how to wright good."

Request of a Bequest

The seventh-graders wrote get-well letters to Joe, a classmate who was an A student. He probably got a little better when he read John's note: "Dear Joe, if you die, can I have your report card?"

26. Holy Days and Holidays

"But you're too big to be an elf."

The More the Merrier

The fourth-graders were learning about the season of Advent. Sister Barbara asked, "Why do you think God waited four thousand years before he sent a Savior?" The creative answer came, "He wanted to stock up on people."

Transportation Problem

With great excitement, Sister explained to her children that at Christmas they were going to celebrate

Jesus' birthday. Baffled, one boy asked, "How are we going to get up there?"

A Christmas Gift

Near Christmas, Sister challenged her class to make as many words as they could out of the letters in "season's greetings." Erika asked, "Can't you change it to "season's greethings" so we can make more words out of it?"

A Giant Elf

During recess and between classes, Sister Jeanne Mary crocheted small items as Christmas gifts for her children. One of her students asked what she was doing. "You never ask Santa's elves what they are doing," Sister replied.

Looking up at his five-foot-nine-inch teacher, the smart little boy pointed out, "You're too big to be an elf."

Christmas Charades

Sister Domicele's fourth-grade class was exceptionally spontaneous. When the students were practicing "O Holy Night," their song for the Christmas program, they complained that one line was really hard. "Which one?" Sister asked. With that, the students stood up and then fell on their knees.

Close!

Sister was reviewing the Christmas story with her little ones. "And where was Baby Jesus born?" she asked. A boy eagerly answered, "In a haystack!"

A Realistic Nativity

The second-graders were intently writing stories. One young lady, whose family had just welcomed a new baby, was smiling brightly as she worked. She wrote about the birth of Jesus. One sentence especially brought a smile to her teacher's face: "When Mary was about to have Baby Jesus, Joseph kept telling her, 'Push, Mary, push, push.'"

Creative Thinking

Reviewing the Nativity story, Sister asked her first-graders how Baby Jesus escaped when the wicked king was trying to kill him. One bright boy said with all sincerity, "He crawled."

Breakfast at Epiphany's?

Sister Barbara asked her seventh-graders if anyone knew what the Epiphany was. Jimmy volunteered an answer: "It's really expensive, like more than glass."

A Vision

A mother told Sister Ann that when her four-year-old son came home from preschool on Ash Wednesday, he declared, "God put ashes on my forehead."

"Oh, and what did God look like?" Mom asked.

"He had white hair and a purple dress."

Bunny Bedtime

At Easter time, Sister Kathleen's parallel teacher, Miss Varygas, told her first-graders that she had Peter Cottontail's phone number. She gave her students letters containing her home phone number and told them that they could call Peter that evening. Her children shared the number with other children. That night her brother played Peter Cottontail and answered very many calls.

Finally, when one little boy called at 10:30 p.m., Miss Varygas herself answered and said, "This is Miss

Varygas. I just put Peter to bed and that's where you should be at this time too!"

The Power of Imagination

When the first-graders returned after Easter vacation, Sister asked one boy if he had seen the Easter bunny. With a solemn look on his face, the youngster replied, "Not really, but I did see something go past the window real fast like this."

He made a hopping movement with his hand.

Trick, No Treat

Sister Jeanne Mary taught her first-graders about St. Nicholas, the holy bishop who secretly left gifts for people. She told the children about the custom of putting shoes outside the door of your room the night before his feast day, December 6, so that St. Nicholas could fill them with goodies.

The next day one little girl came to school with a note: "Dear Sister, please excuse Ann for wearing tennis shoes today. Last night she put her good school shoes outside and it rained."

Mercy

For Mother's Day, the children were making gifts by pasting tissue squares onto the large letters of the word *Mom*. When it was almost time for lunch, everyone was finished except Karen. Sister Marian offered to help her. As they worked, Sister could tell that Karen was not pleased with her assistance. Sister remarked, "I'm sorry, Karen. I can see that I'm not doing this as well as you are."

Karen looked up at Sister with a sweet smile and said, "I forgive you, Sister!"

Secret Identity

For Easter, the pastor asked Sister Kathleen, a pastoral associate, if she would put on a rabbit costume and distribute candy to the school children. Swallowing her pride, Sister donned ears and a bunny suit and drew whiskers on her face. After delivering Easter treats, Sister overhead one tot say to her mom, "I didn't know that Sister Kathleen was the Easter bunny."

27. Misunderstandings

"Mommy, you woke me up at the wrong six o'clock!"

School, Zoo, or Morgue?

The principal, in her announcements to the school, stated that the forms the teachers had distributed were to be taken home and filled out. She concluded by saying, "The deadline is Friday."

A little boy dutifully brought the form home to his mother and then broke the exciting news: "Friday there's going to be a dead lion in school! Mom, what's a dead lion doing in school?"

A Privileged Preschooler

Sister Emilia entertained the other sisters with a story about her friend's little niece. The child had told a classmate at her preschool to shut up. The teacher immediately instructed all the children, "No one else in this class is ever to tell another child to shut up."

After school, when the mother of the little girl asked how the day went, the girl reported, "The teacher said I'm the only one who can say 'Shut up.'"

A Major Difference

On the playground, a teacher praised a primary-level boy for observing a certain school policy. He ran to his own teacher and excitedly told her that another sister wanted to condemn him. (Commend, maybe?)

The Butcher

The primary class was discussing their parents' jobs.

"And what does your daddy do?" the teacher asked a little girl.

She replied, "He makes bacon."

"Oh, really? And how does he do that?" the teacher asked.

"I don't know, but every morning my mom says good-bye and tells him to bring home the bacon."

Gardening Secrets

The school was undergoing an evaluation. As part of the process, the students were asked to write answers to questions on an evaluation sheet. In response to the question, "What do you think of your school plant?" one child wrote, "There are many plants in our school. I don't know which one is the school plant."

School Rules Rule

A child from the Montessori school insisted on wearing her coat to school even though it was a very warm autumn day. Her mother could not understand why, until the little one explained, "I have to hang up my coat as soon as I get to school."

Miniature Sisters

Sister was introducing the new fund-raiser to her youngsters. They would be raising money to support the work of the Little Sisters of the Poor. One little boy had a puzzled expression on his face.

"Just how big are these Little Sisters?" he queried.

Blind Obedience

John, a sophomore, had to stay after school for detention. Sister Alice put him to work in the classroom. It was time to change the papers on the small bulletin board in the back of the room. "John," Sister said, "would you please take down that bulletin board." Unfamiliar with that expression, John walked to the back of the room and wrenched the entire bulletin board off the wall!

Tabled

In one school, the cafeteria tables folded into the walls to convert the room into a large social hall. A watchful teacher supervising the lunch period noticed that every day one group of first-graders rushed through their lunch. On investigating, she discovered that they were afraid of being folded into the walls with the tables.

Mommy's Mistake

One mother reported that on the first morning of school her kindergartener greeted her with his hands planted on his hips and a big frown on his face. He scolded her, "Mommy, you woke me up at the wrong six o'clock!"

Dead or Alive

Mom and Dad were going to a wake and decided to take four-year-old Tommy. They thought he was old enough for this experience. On the way home, Tommy mused, "It's hard to be dead."

"Why do you say that?" Dad asked.

"Because you have to hold your breath so long," Tommy replied.

28. Hodgepodge

"We have to do work, and your mommy
has to do work. So let's get to work."

Tuition by the Hour

On the first day of school, a first-grader who was accustomed to half days in kindergarten was concerned. He asked, "Sister, do I have to pay extra to stay for the afternoon?"

A Quick Cure

One morning a few days after school started, John, a first-grader, had an attack of school phobia. He cried and cried for his mommy and refused to go into the classroom. In desperation, Sister Lisa, the principal, called for another first-grade boy who had suffered such an attack on the first day of school. She asked him, "Remember how you had a hard time leaving your mother? What could John do?"

Both boys sat down on the steps. The boy who had recovered counseled John, "We have to do work, and your mommy has to do work. So let's get to work."

With that, the two boys got up and walked into the classroom.

All What?

The parish priest liked to wear pullover sweaters. While visiting Sister Sharon's second-grade class, he was attracted to one fellow's sweater.

"Do you think I could borrow your sweater some-time?" Father teased the boy.

"Sure," the lad generously responded. "One size fits all."

Telltale Purple

Seeing a purple line around the upper lip of one little boy, Sister remarked, "Just by looking at you, I can tell you had grape juice for breakfast."

"No, I didn't," the boy stated. Then the light dawned. "It must be the Kool-Aid I had yesterday."

A New Emily Post

Sister Barbara was teaching her seventh-graders the etiquette rules for making introductions, such as the younger person is presented to the older one and the less important is presented to the more important. Donna shared her own rule with her classmates: "I go by the wrinkles."

A Recycled Library

The school library project involved a number of fund-raisers to procure money for books. One Sunday an announcement in the church bulletin read, "School News: We are building our library from rags and empty pop bottles. Please bring these discarded items to the church lounge."

The Cinderella Desk

One day a new student was assigned to Sister Immaculee's third grade. There were no more desks except for one in storage that left much to be desired. Its legs were bent, the wood was scarred, and the metal was rusted. No student would want such a desk and would probably complain if it became his or her designated seat.

Then Sister had a brilliant idea. She introduced the desk to the class as the honor desk. The student who made the biggest improvement each week could sit in that desk the following week. For the rest of the year, the children vied to be the student privileged to occupy that shabby desk.

Modern Teens

Sister Joela passed out playing cards to form her students into groups of four. The twos would be in one group, the threes in another, and so on. "Don't damage these cards or put them in your backpacks," she warned. "I use them to play a couple games of solitaire at night."

A young man raised his hand and asked, "How do you do that?"

Sister began to explain, "There are seven piles of cards in a row."

The boy interrupted, "I know how to play solitaire, but how do you play it without a computer?"